FAO FOOD AND NUTRITION PAPER 14/10

manuals
of food quality control
10. training in mycotoxins analysis

FOOD AND AGRICULTURE ORGANIZATION OF THE UNITED NATIONS
ROME, 1990

M-82

ISBN 92-5-102947-4

FOREWORD

In most developing countries, agriculture is the back-bone of the economy and export crops are greatly depended upon as a source of foreign exchange to finance productive activities and other essential services.

Most of these crops are cereals and oil seeds that are highly susceptible to fungal growth and mycotoxin production. The mycotoxins are not only hazardous to consumer health but also affect food quality resulting in huge economic losses for these countries.

This Manual was prepared for, and on behalf of, the Food and Agriculture Organization of the United Nations to provide a training package for the National Governments of developing countries that are seeking to improve their mycotoxin prevention and monitoring programmes. The Manual is intended for training at national and regional levels.

FAO wishes to acknowledge the efforts of Mr. H.P. van Egmond from the Laboratory for Residue Analysis, National Institute of Public Health and Environmental Hygiene, Bilthoven, The Netherlands, who was responsible for the preparation of the text. Part of the text of section III have been copied, with permission of the publishers, from the article "Determination of Mycotoxins" by H.P. Van Egmond, which appeared in "Developments in Food Analysis Techniques III", R.D. King (editor), Applied Science Publishers Ltd., Barking, Essex, England (1984), 99-144.

J.W. Dickens (North Carolina State University, Raleigh, NC, USA) and E. Mulders (CIVO-YNO, Zeist, The Netherlands) provided figures 9-13 and figure 26 respectively.

The Typing Officer, Karen Pool, the Layout Department and the Photography Department of the National Institute of Public Health and Environmental Hygiene are also gratefully acknowledged for their contributions to this Manual.

This publication is available to persons and organizations. A list of publications and papers on mycotoxins published by FAO is given at the end of this Manual. Comments on suggestions for possible future editions of this publication should be sent to:

The Chief
Food Quality and Standards Service
Food Policy and Nutrition Division
Food and Agriculture Organization of the United Nations
00100 Rome, Italy

SPECIAL NOTE

The methods and analytical procedures described in this Manual are designed to be carried out by properly trained personnel in a suitably equipped laboratory. In common with many laboratory procedures, the methods quoted frequently involve hazardous materials.

For the correct and safe execution of these methods, it is essential that laboratory personnel follow standard safety procedures for the handling of hazardous materials.

While the greatest care has been exercised in the preparation of this information, FAO expressly disclaims any liability to users of these procedures for consequential damages of any kind arising out of or connected with their use.

The methods are also not to be regarded as official because of their inclusion in this Manual. They are simply methods which have been found by experience to be usable in the average laboratory.

TABLE OF CONTENTS

I PURPOSE AND SCOPE

Over a number of years, the Food Quality and Standards Service of FAO has been assisting developing countries in strengthening their capabilities to prevent and control the contamination of food by mycotoxins, particularly aflatoxins. During this time, several international training courses and conferences were organized. The courses were held on an **ad hoc** basis, with invited consultants and lecturers providing their own material. However it was felt that a more uniform approach would be desired, while still retaining a certain degree of flexibility and country specificity. The preparation of a core syllabus and curriculum for a training package that would suit the needs of these countries was therefore undertaken.

This Manual is designed to cover courses of about three weeks duration and is directed towards training analysts in developing countries. Emphasis has been placed on analysis for aflatoxins in foods and feeds.

II ORGANIZATIONAL ASPECTS OF TRAINING COURSES

1. General

The establishment of a workable situation for a mycotoxin training course, requires attention be paid to a number of organizational aspects. It is essential that the course leader gets a detailed picture of the facilities at the proposed training site, and that he is informed about the budget available for procuring additonal supplies at an early stage. If time and resources allow, it would be best for the course leader to visit the proposed site shortly after his recruitment, possibly six months prior to the planned course date, to estimate its suitability for the course, to identify possible problems, to suggest adaptations, to make contact with the local authorities and to order the needed supplementary supplies. In addition to or instead of a personal visit questionnaire forms can be used, to get an idea of the situation at the proposed training site (see Annex I B).

2. Laboratory facilities

For an analytical training course on mycotoxins, a simple classroom is needed, where lectures and theory can be given, and a laboratory, where experimental work can be carried out. The laboratory must have:

- A consistent supply of water and electricity
- At least one fume-hood
- The possibility to exclude daylight
- Facilities for airconditioning in hot and humid climatic zones
- Ample bench-space for each participant
- Waste disposal facilities

A questionnaire according to model B (see Annex I) may be helpful in estimating the suitability of laboratory facilities.

3. Basic reagents and equipment

Although emphasis is put in these training documents on methods of analysis for aflatoxins, that are relatively easy to perform, it is impossible to carry out aflatoxin assays without a minimum of reagents and equipment. A questionnaire according to model C (see Annex I) may be helpful in finding out if essential supplies are available. Detailed lists of specific reagents and equipment for some laboratory procedures are given in section 4.

4. Educational level of participants

The official educational degrees in various developing countries are difficult to evaluate, especially for outsiders, but in general a high school level education is required for participation in mycotoxin training courses. Experience in mycotoxin assays is not a prerequisite. However, to gain full benefit of a three week training course requires some experience in analytical chemistry, preferably in trace analysis. A questionnaire according to model A (Annex I) may be used to obtain some information about the participants.

5. Experiences with previous courses

Various aflatoxin training courses have been held in African and other countries between 1982 and 1988. The following points drawn from practical experiences with earlier courses are worth mentioning, as they can be instructive when programming activities of future mycotoxin training courses in developing countries.

a. A period of two weeks is a minimum for unexperienced analysts to become familiar with thin larger chromatographic determination of aflatoxins in foods and feeds. If other techniques, such as enzyme-linked immunosorbent assay would also be taught and practiced, a three week period would be preferable.

b. A group of 6 trainees per teacher is considered to be a maximum to guarantee the necessary personal attention. For reasons of efficiency, presence of a local assistant at the laboratory where the course is held, would be required.   If the course is national in scope, it is desirable that participants from different Institutions take part.   This might stimulate future cooperation between these Institutions, which may have different tasks, responsibilities and facilities.

c. Chemicals and simple equipment, not available at the training site, but indispensable for the training course, should be bought in Europe or elsewhere and shipped to the developing country by airfreight, as this means of transport was found to be safe and the easiest to control. (e.g. Prices of chemicals that would have been bought in Nairobi in 1984, were 40% higher than prices for the same chemicals bought in Europe, airfreight inclusive). Where possible, consignments should be sent two months in advance of the course date to allow time for handling local formalities, which can be very time-consuming.   The consignments should be stored safely at the destination and left unopened until arrival of the course leader.

d. The course leader should arrive at the training site 3-5 working days before the opening date of the training course. This would allow a minimum time for acclimatisation and handling inevitable administrative affairs and organizational matters.

e. It is not uncommon to find some trainees who cannot perform simple arithmetic calculations. In such instances some homework exercises would be most helpful.   Draft exercises have been included in Annex II.

f. Working in the field of analytical chemistry, and especially trace analysis, demands extreme care and neatness in the laboratory as well as a sound amount of self-criticism. The attitude of the trainees towards these requirements will probably need some encouragement, even though they may show great interest and willingness to take full advantage of the course.

g. At the end of a training course an evaluation should be made in which the comments of the participants should be included. A simple questionnaire such as model E in Annex I may be used to obtain this information.

III   MYCOTOXINS, SIGNIFICANCE AND ANALYSIS

1.   Introduction

Mycotoxins may be defined as metabolites of fungi, which evoke pathological changes in man and animals. The term "mycotoxin" is derived from the Greek words "mykes" (fungus) and "toksikon" (poison). Mycotoxicoses may be defined as the toxicity syndromes resulting from the intake of mycotoxins by man and animals, usually by ingestion.

The diseases caused by mycotoxins have been known for a long time. The first recognized mycotoxicosis was probably ergotism, a disease, characterized by necrosis and gangrene and better known in the Middle Ages in Europe under the name "Holy Fire", which was caused by the intake of grain contaminated with sclerotia of Claviceps purpurea.

Another mycotoxicosis, recognized to have seriously affected human populations is Alimentary Toxic Aleukia (ATA). The symptoms in man take on many aspects, including leukopenia, necrotic lesions of the oral cavity, the oesophagus and stomach, sepsis, haemorrhagic diathesis and exhaustion of the bone marrow. The disease was induced by eating overwintered mouldy grain and occurred in many areas in Russia, especially during World War II. The fungi responsible for these accidents belong to the genera Fusarium and Cladosporium.

In Japan, toxicity associated with yellow coloured mouldy rice has been a problem, especially after World War II, when rice had to be imported from various countries. The intake of "yellow rice" by man caused vomiting, convulsions and ascending paralysis. Death could also occur within 1–3 days after the first signs of the disease appeared. The toxin producing fungi in yellow rice belong to the genus Penicillium.

Despite the fore-mentioned examples of mycotoxin-caused diseases in man, mycotoxicoses remained the "neglected diseases" until the early 1960's, when this attitude changed drastically by the outbreak of Turkey X Disease in Great Britain. Within a few months more than 100,000 turkeys died, mainly in East Anglia and southern England. In addition, the death of thousands of ducklings and young pheasants was reported (Asplin, 1961). The appearance of Turkey X Disease led to a multi-disciplinary approach to investigate the cause of the problem. These efforts were successful and the cause of the disease was traced to a toxic factor occurring in the Brazilian goundnut meal which was used as a protein source in the feed of those affected poultry. The toxic factor seemed to be produced by two fungi, Aspergillus parasiticus and Aspergillus flavus, hence, the name "aflatoxin" was given to it, an acronym derived from the name of the second mentioned fungus. Further elucidation of the toxic factor demonstrated that the material could be separated chromatographically into four distinct spots. All four components have been given the name "aflatoxins" in order to identify their generic origin. Distinction of the four substances was made on the basis of their fluorescent colour with subscripts relating to their relative chromatographic mobility. Later on it became clear that the group of aflatoxins consists of at least 17 closely related compounds.

In the two decades following the outbreak of Turkey X disease, a wealth of information about aflatoxins has been produced and many other mycotoxins have also been isolated and characterized. At present over 200 different mycotoxins are known, showing a large variety of chemical structures. Examples of a few of these structures are shown in Figure 1.

The many different mycotoxins have demonstrated different biological effects in laboratory animals: acute toxic, mutagenic, carcinogenic, teratogenic, hallucinogenic, emetic and oestrogenic.

Humans and animals may be exposed to mycotoxins through ingestion of toxin-contaminated food and feed, inhalation or skin-contact.

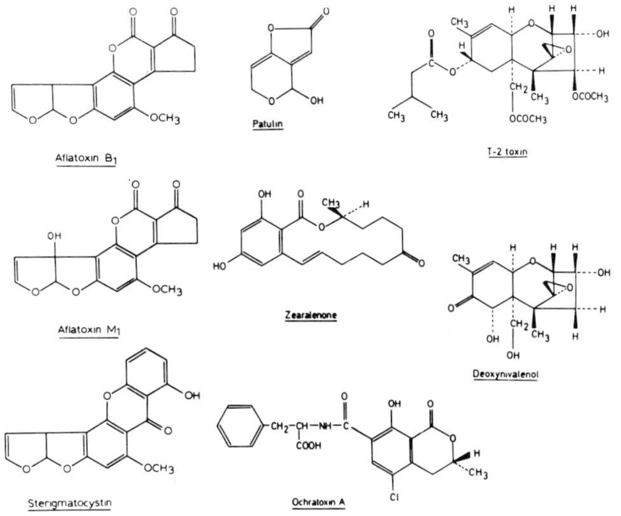

Figure 1. Chemical structures of some mycotoxins

The presence of mycotoxins in human food may be the result of:

a. Direct fungal contamination of agricultural crops in the field, raw materials, manufactured products and final products. An example of field spoilage is the occurrence of aflatoxins in peanuts, an important crop in many developing countries. An example of spoilage of a semi-manufactured product is the occurrence of sterigmatocystin in cheese.

b. The contamination of animal products caused by contamination of the feedstuff consumed by the animal. An example is the contamination of milk and dairy products with the 4-hydroxy derivative of aflatoxin B1, called aflatoxin M1, a metabolite formed through the dairy cow after ingestion of feed contaminated with aflatoxin B1 (Allcroft,1963). These facts have led many countries to exact legal measures to control mycotoxin contamination in foods as well as in animal feeds (see section III.4). Developing countries that have significant exports of animal feeds and feed ingredients to the industrialized world should recognize the importance of controlling aflatoxin levels not only in foodstuffs, but in animal feedstuffs as well.

For surveys, monitoring and enforcement programmes, effective methods of analysis are needed. The simplicity of the method will influence the amount of data that will be generated and the practicality of the ultimate control measures consequently taken. It may be clear that the availability of methods of analysis plays a keyrole in survey and research programmes. Nevertheless, efficient tackling of the mycotoxin problem requires a multidisciplinary approach, in which mycology, toxicology and chemistry each play a role of major importance. In the following sections, however, mycological and toxicological aspects are treated in minor detail. Emphasis is placed on analysis for mycotoxins in particular aflatoxins, a group of highly carcinogenic mycotoxins, which have been intensively investigated.

2. Fungal growth and toxin production

Toxinogenic moulds may invade agricultural products during plant growth, during harvest and afterwards. Contamination occurs with spores or conidia and mycelium fragments from the environment. The presence of large numbers of spores or conidia and mycelium fragments in products that are not visibly mouldy can point to a general contamination of the environment on the one hand, or to the processing of mouldy raw material on the other. During processing, the fungi may be inactivated and are no longer viable. Fungal growth only occurs under favourable conditions. Fungi need various nutrients for their energy needs and for making macro-molecules, such as proteins and DNA. Since fungi cannot synthesize carbohydrates the substrate should contain these compounds, although fungi can grow in a substrate rich in proteins by using amino acids as a carbon source. Organic nitrogen compounds can be assimilated by all fungi, whereas inorganic compounds can only be assimilated by a limited number of species. Certain vitamins must be present in the substrate, others can be synthesized, depending on the species. Almost all foodstuffs contain the above mentioned nutrients and can, therefore, serve as substrate.

A large number of metabolites are formed during the breakdown of carbohydrates. Among these are those that are toxic for humans and animals (the mycotoxins) and those that are toxic for micro-organisms (the antibiotics). The number of fungi, known to produce mycotoxins is about 150. In Table 1 a few examples are given of some well-known moulds and their mycotoxins (see also Figure 1 for structural formulae of the mentioned mycotoxin.

Table 1

Toxigenic moulds and their toxins

Fungal Species	Toxins
Aspergillus flavus	aflatoxins
Aspergillus versicolor	sterigmatocystin
Penicillium verrucosum	ochratoxins
Fusarium roseum	zearalenone
Fusarium tricinctum	trichothecenes

In addition to the presence of nutrients, the most important factors for growth and mycotoxin production are oxygen, temperature and water activity. Most fungi need oxygen, although some can grow under anaerobic conditions by using a fermentation process in which ethanol and organic acids are formed. The minimum, optimum and maximum temperatures for growth may differ largely for the various species. Some species may grow below 0 C, others have a minimum of 10 C. Most of the Penicillia have a lower minimal temperature range than the Aspergilli. The optimal temperature is 25-30 C for most Penicillia and 30-40 C for most Aspergilli, temperature ranges that will often be met in tropical countries. Various Fusarium species have optimal temperature ranges of 8-15 C, and they occur in the moderate climatic zones.

Water activity (aW) has taken the place of moisture content as the most useful expression of the availability of water for growth of micro-organisms (Scott, 1957). Figure 2 describes the various concepts (Northolt, 1984). The relative humidity is used for the atmosphere. The equilibrium relative humidity or the equilibrium relative water vapour pressure concerns the atmosphere in a closed space, where the water vapour pressure is in equilibrium with the humidity of the stored material. The aW equals the quotient of the water vapour pressure around the food, when this is in equilibrium with the humidity of the food, and the vapour pressure of pure water at the same temperature. Fungi generally have a much lower minimal aW than bacteria. This explains why many products free of spoilage by bacteria can be spoiled by fungi. Fungal growth can be prevented by drying agricultural products to a level below 0.65 aW and keeping it under this level. In figure 3 a summary of the conditions of aW and temperature for growth of some fungal species and production of mycotoxins is given (Northolt, 1982). It should be noted that the aW and temperature ranges shown encompass the lowest and highest values obtained with the various strains and substrates. Aflatoxin B1 can be produced at conditions of aW and temperature which are close to the minimum aW and temperature for growth. Patulin and ochratoxin A (see Fig. 1) are produced within a smaller range of aW and temperature compared with that for growth. However, the production of patulin appears to be confined to substrates at a high aW.

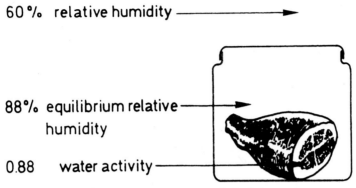

Figure 2. Different parameters related to water vapour (after Northolt, 1984)

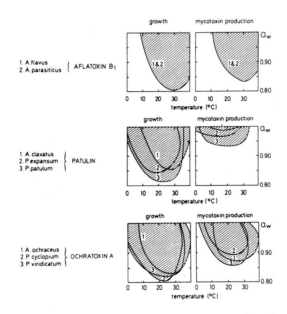

Figure 3. Conditions of water activity (a_w) and temperature favourable (shaded area) for growth and mycotoxin production by different species (after Northolt, 1981).

The Codex Alimentarius Committee on Food Hygiene has proposed an aW standard of 0.70 for peanuts to prevent contamination with aflatoxins. The aW standard of 0.70 is also useful for safe storage of other agricultural products. However, the introduction of aW standards is hampered because of either the complexity and price or the need of frequent calibration of the aW measuring devices (dewpoint meters). Therefore Northolt (1982) developed a simple method for testing the water activity of foods, which can be applied under field circumstances, the so-called salt crystal liquefaction test. The method is based on the property of salt crystals to attract water vapour and to liquefy if the water vapour pressure of the surrounding air exceeds water vapour pressure of a saturated solution of the salt. The latter is specific for the various kinds of salts, and is mostly written as the equilibrium relative water vapour or the aW of the salt. The test is simply carried out by putting a mixture of dry crystals and the food sample in a jar. If the aW of the food sample is higher than the aW of the salt, the crystals will liquefy within a few hours, a phenomenon, which can easily be observed by the human eye. For checking the aW of peanuts, $CuCl_2.H_2O$ crystals are used, which liquefy at aW = ca 0.70 (See also section IV-1 for the practical performance of the test). When 50% or more of the crystals are liquefied the test result is regarded as positive .

The salt crystal liquefaction test is an indirect physical field test that indicates only the possibility of presence of one or more mycotoxins. Next to this type of tests, many methods of analysis exist to detect and determine the actual presence of one or more mycotoxins in the commodity to be inspected. These will be discussed in section III-6.

3. Occurrence and toxicity

Mycotoxin contamination of foods and feeds highly depends on environmental conditions that lead to mould growth and toxin production. Data about incidence and levels of contamination are limited by many factors, including the resources to conduct surveys, the availability of laboratory facilities to carry out analyses, the sampling procedure(s) used, the reliability and sensitivity of the analytical methods used and the capabilities of the analyst(s). Nevertheless there have appeared numerous publications about the occurrence of various mycotoxins in foods and feeds, since the discovery of the aflatoxins in the early 1960's. Probably no edible substance can be regarded as absolutely safe from possible mycotoxin contamination, and mycotoxin production can occur in the field, during harvest, processing, storage and shipment of a given commodity. It would be impossible and inappropriate to review all the occurrence data here. Some occurrence data are summarized in "Environmental Health Criteria Document 11: Mycotoxins" (WHO, 1980). Most of the data refer to the notorious aflatoxins, which particularly occur in groundnuts and groundnut products, maize and other grains, such as rice, wheat, sorghum and millet in quantities from the sub mcg/kg to the mg/kg range. In many countries, tolerance levels for aflatoxins in foodstuffs are in the range of 5-25 mcg/kg, in feedstuffs they are often higher (see section III-4.).

The acute and chronic effects of aflatoxin exposure have been well studied and some detailed reviews should be consulted for in-depth information (Heathcote, 1978) (Stoloff, 1977). Aflatoxin B1 is the most toxic followed by aflatoxins G1, B2 and G2 in order of decreasing potency. LD50 values in one day-old ducklings were for these mycotoxins 0.36, 0.78, 1.70 and 3.45 mg/kg body weight respectively (Carnaghan, 1963). The suscept bility of animals to aflatoxins varies from species to species, with rabbits, ducklings, pigs, trout and rats being moderately susceptible, whereas mice, hamsters and chicks are relatively resistant. Acute aflatoxicoses results in widespread hemorrhage, fatty accumulation in the liver and death.

Even more alarming than the facts about the acute effects of aflatoxins was the finding that aflatoxin B1 is a very potent hepatocarcinogen in the rat (Butler, 1968), and in all other species of laboratory animals tested (Wogan, 1973). The liver tumorigenicity of aflatoxin B1 in various strains of rats is summarized in Table 2.

Primary liver cancer is one of the most prevalent human cancers in the developing countries. Epidemiological studies carried out in the 1970's offer statistical support for the association between the incidence of hepatocellular carcinoma and consumption of foods contaminated with aflatoxin. In these studies it was assumed legitimate to compare current exposure to aflatoxin with present cancer rates, as observations were limited to stable rural populations with diet, storage and cooking habits that had not changed over the recent past (Dil, 1986). It is now believed that there are synergistic effects between aflatoxin and hepatitis B virus infection causing primary liver cancer. This multifactorial etiology theory is rapidly gaining support from recent findings of molecular genetic investigations on the mechanisms of hepatocarcinogenesis (Hsieh, 1986). Evidence for a very limited hepatocarcinogenic effect in humans of aflatoxin acting in isolation is mounting (Van Rensburg, 1986).

Table 2

Liver cancer data from aflatoxin B1 (AFB) feeding studies with rats (after Hsieh, 1986):

Study No.	Strain of rats	AFB in diet (mcg/kg)	Incidence of liver cancer	Reference
I	Fischer	0	0/18 (0)	Wogan (1974)
		1	2/22 (0.09)	
		5	1/22 (0.05)	
		15	4/21 (0.19)	
		50	20/25 (0.80)	
		100	28/28 (1.0)	
II	Fischer	0	0/16 (0)	Nixon (1974)
		20	5/13 (0.38)	
III	Wistar	0	0/17 (0)	
		20	0/20 (0)	
		100	7/17 (0.41)	
IV	Porton	0	0/46 (0)	Butler (1968)
		100	17/26 (0.47)	
		500	25/25 (1.0)	
V	USC	0	0/9 (0)	Alfin-Slater (1969)
		1	0/16 (0)	
		10	0/10 (0)	

Acute and chronic effects of some other major mycotoxins (see Fig. 1) have also been studied and reported. Ochratoxin A has been shown to be a potent nephrotoxin in all species of animals tested, including birds, fish and mammals (Krogh, 1977). There is a hypothesis that ochratoxin A is associated with Balkan endemic nephropathy, a renal disease observed in some areas of the Balkan countries (Krogh, 1974). Recently also reports about the carcinogenicity of ochratoxin A in mice were published (Bendele, 1985). Patulin is rather an indicator of bad manufacturing practices (use of mouldy raw materials) than a serious threat to human and animal health, as recent subacute and semi-chronic toxicity studies revealed (Speyers, 1987, 1988). Nevertheless there are 8 countries with official tolerances for patulin (Van Egmond, 1987). Sterigmatocystin is a carcinogen, occasionally occurring in grains and in the outer rim of hard cheeses. The toxin has a chemical structure related to the aflatoxins. Of the trichothecenes, T-2 toxin and deoxynivalenol attract most attention. These compounds exhibit a wide range of toxic effects in experimental animals including feed refusal, vomiting, diarrhea and severe hemorrhage. These compounds are also severely teratogenic and they interfere with the immune system.

For the developing countries the aflatoxins are the most important mycotoxins from the point of view of occurrence, toxicity and economy. The favourable climatic conditions for fungal growth and toxin production in foods and food ingredients and the improper methods of handling foods make it likely that a part of their populations are exposed to some level of aflatoxin intoxication. The problem of reducing the risk of exposure to aflatoxins is far more difficult than it is in the developed countries. At the present time, at least, for some of these people avoidance of all foodstuffs contaminated with aflatoxins is almost impossible.

Coupled to the health hazards of mycotoxins in general and aflatoxins in particular is the negative economic impact for these countries. In most of them, harvest and post-harvest technologies which would prevent mould growth and mycotoxin production are sometimes inadequate or simply lacking. The economic consequences for such nations exporting food crops and other products to countries with effective contamination control programmes and enforced food quality control practices, can be devastating. The presence of mycotoxins in feeds can also adversely affect animal productivity. Assuming a reduction in weight of 3% in broilers due to low levels of mycotoxins, Hesseltine (1986) estimated an annual loss of more than 140 million U.S. dollars. These and other aspects of mycotoxin regulations are discussed in section 4.

4. Limits and regulations

The hazards to humans or animals from ingestion of mycotoxin contaminated agricultural commodities has led many countries to establish measures to control the contamination of foodstuffs and animal feedstuffs.

Various factors play a role in establishing limits and regulations for mycotoxins. These are:

a. Survey data: The availability of data on occurrence, indicates which commodities should be considered for legal action. Also these data will allow an estimate of the effects of enforcement on the availability of food, including animal products, and of feed. However, in developing countries where the food supply is already limited drastic legal measures might lead to lack of food and to higher prices.

b. Toxicological data: Without toxicological information there can be no proper assessment of whether or not the substance in question is indeed hazardous. Measures are most logically taken on the basis of specific toxicological effects, except when cancer is the basis for concern as is the case with aflatoxins. The current assumption is that there is no threshold level for aflatoxins below which some effects cannot occur and that, therefore, any small dose will cause a proportionally small probability of inducing some effect. A zero tolerance would be appropriate then, but the problem is that aflatoxins are natural contaminants which cannot be eliminated completely without outlawing the susceptible food or feed. This makes regulatory judgements particularly difficult.

c. Methods of analysis: To make inspection of commodities possible, accurate methods of analysis have to be available. If reliable methods of analysis do not exist, the fulfillment of established tolerances is not possible. It should also be borne in mind that in fact a tolerance cannot be lower than the actual limit of detection of the method of analysis used.

d. Mycotoxin distribution: The distribution of the mycotoxin(s) in the products may pose very difficult problems in establishing regulatory criteria. If such a distribution is non-homogeneous, as is the case with aflatoxins in peanuts, there is a good chance that the mycotoxin concentration in the lot to be inspected will be wrongly estimated, due to the difficulties in representative sampling. The risk to both consumer and producer must be considered when establishing sampling and analysis criteria for peanuts (see section 5).

e. Legislation: Finally the regulations in force in other countries with which trade-contacts exist, have to be considered and, if possible, brought into harmony with the legislation under consideration. Despite their necessity, regulations constitute a handicap to international trade, since they may create:

- difficulties for exporting countries finding markets for their products.

- difficulties for importing countries in obtaining supplies of
  essential commodities as food grains and animal feedstuffs.

It will be clear that there is no simple formula for weighing these factors. Common sense is the major factor for reaching decision. Public Health officials are confronted with a complex problem: mycotoxins, and particularly aflatoxins should be excluded from

11

food as far as possible, but since the substances are present in foods as natural contaminants the exposure to man cannot be completely prevented. It follows therefore that exposure of the population to some level of aflatoxins must be tolerated. The adoption of regulations for aflatoxin control has been a process of continuous development in some countries. For most countries background information on the decisions taken in establishing tolerances have not been made public. An exception is the USA, where all problems and difficulties have been published so that the rationale behind the decisions taken is known (Stoloff, 1980)

In 1981 an attempt was made to get an overview of world-wide mycotoxin legislation resulting in a publication by Schuller (1983) on the subject. This compilation contains information about mycotoxin legislation in 46 countries. Since 1981, mycotoxin regulations have been changed, expanded or created in various countries. Therefore an updated document was prepared for the Second Joint FAO/WHO/UNEP International Conference on Mycotoxins which reflects the situation as per May 1987 (Van Egmond, Bangkok, 1987). The updated document contains information about specific regulations or detailed proposals for regulations on mycotoxins in 56 countries. The fact that many countries have not enacted specific legislation does not necessarily mean they are unaware of the problem, or that the problem does not exist in their country. Many countries rely on general legislation such as: "the product shall be free from micro organisms capable of development under normal conditions of storage and shall not contain any substances originating from micro organisms in amounts which may present a hazard to health".

In the FAO working documents Myc 87/9.1 and Myc 87/9.2 details are given about worldwide tolerances, legal bases, responsible authorities, status of methods of sampling and analysis and disposition of commodities containing inadmissible amounts of mycotoxins. The information concerns aflatoxins in foodstuffs, aflatoxin M1 in dairy products, aflatoxins in animal feedstuffs and other mycotoxins in foodstuffs and feedstuffs. Selected information about the various tolerances has been summarized in the form of frequency distributions in Figures 4-8 With respect to these Figures the following restrictions and simplifications were made in order to make comparisons possible.

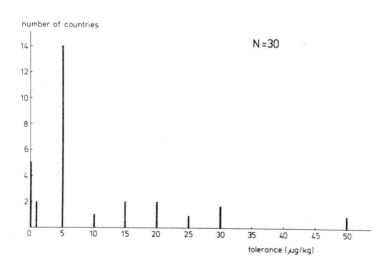

Figure 4. Frequency distribution of tolerated (in force and proposed) amounts of aflatoxin B$_1$ in foodstuffs in various countries.

In those cases, where countries had different aflatoxin tolerances for different products, the tolerance for the "major" foodstuff(s) (often peanut product(s)) was taken, which occasionally may have been a subjective choice. Countries that had indicated a zero tolerance for the sum of aflatoxins B1, B2, G1 and G2 were automatically taken as to have a zero tolerance for aflatoxin B1, if this was not specified separately.

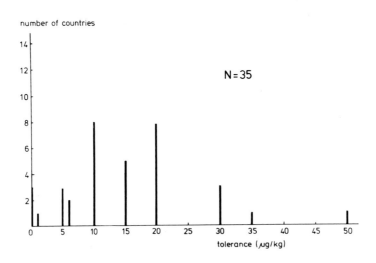

Figure 5. Frequency distribution of tolerated (in force and proposed) amounts of the sum of aflatoxins $B_1+B_2+G_1+G_2$ in foodstuffs in various countries.

In those cases, where countries had different aflatoxin tolerances for different products, the tolerance for the "major" foodstuff(s) (often peanut product(s)) was taken, which occasionally may have been a subjective choice. Tolerances for the sum of aflatoxin B1 and other aflatoxins were taken as tolerances for the sum of aflatoxins B1, B2, G1 and G2.

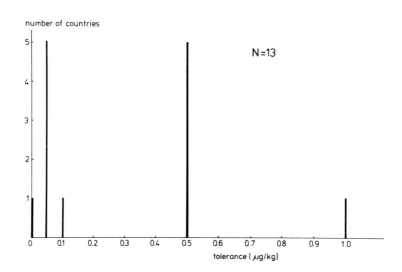

Figure 6. Frequency distribution of tolerated (in force and proposed) amounts of aflatoxin M_1 in milk in various countries.

Only tolerances for aflatoxin M1 in liquid milk (not for specified milk-containing products, such as infant foods) were included.

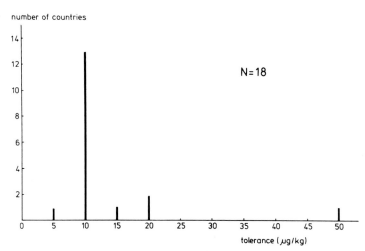

Figure 7. Frequency distribution of tolerated (in force and proposed) amounts of aflatoxin B_1 in feedstuffs (for dairy cattle) in various countries.

Only tolerances for aflatoxin B1 in feeds for dairy cattle (or animal feeds in general, if not more specific) were included.

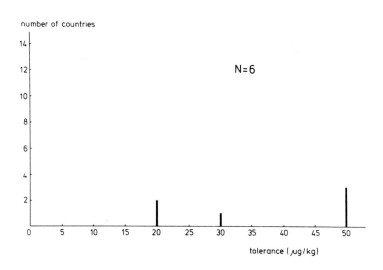

Figure 8. Frequency distribution of tolerated (in force and proposed) amounts of aflatoxins $B_1+B_2+G_1+G_2$ in feedstuffs (for dairy cattle) in various countries.

See comments with figure 4.

From Figure 4, it can be seen that the tolerance level for aflatoxin B1 of 5 mcg/kg is most often applied by drafters of aflatoxin regulations for foodstuffs. In those countries that apply limits for the sum of the aflatoxins, such as uniformity in tolerance values does not occur (Figure 5). It is debatable, whether or not a tolerance for the sum of the aflatoxins, which requires more analytical work than for aflatoxin B1 alone, contributes significantly to better protection of Public Health than a tolerance for aflatoxin B1 alone. Aflatoxin B1 is the most important of the aflatoxins, considered from both the viewpoints of toxicology and occurrence. It is unlikely that commodities will contain aflatoxins B2, G1 and G2 and not aflatoxin B1, whereas the concentration of the sum of the aflatoxins B2, G1 and G2 is generally less than the concentration of aflatoxin B1 alone (Van Egmond, unpublished data).

The frequency distribution of Figure 6 shows that for aflatoxin M1 in milk two major tolerance peaks occur, 0.05 and 0.5 mcg/kg. It is indeed amazing to notice these large differences in M1-tolerances between some Western European countries (0.05 mcg/kg) and some American countries, the USSR and Czechoslovakia (0.5 mcg/kg). The trend in Western European countries to establish tolerances for aflatoxin M1 in milk, at a level of 0.05 mcg/kg, has led to a tightening in the EC-feedstuff regulations for aflatoxin B1 in complementary feedstuffs for dairy cattle to 10 mcg/kg in 1984 (See major peak at 10 mcg/kg in Figure 7). Another recent development in Community legislation is the introduction of a tolerance for aflatoxin B1 in feedstuff ingredients at 200 mcg/kg, a measure which will obtain legal status by the end of 1988. The developments in international mycotoxin regulations may lead to increasing problems for the developing countries, as they are obliged to establish export limits that meet their customers requirements.

The aflatoxins form the major group of mycotoxins for which regulations exist. However 15 countries also had proposed or actual tolerances for other mycotoxins in 1987. These include patulin, ochratoxin A, deoxynivalenol, T-2 toxin and zearalenone (see Figure 1) and the lesser known mycotoxins chetomyotoxin, stachiobotriotoxin and phomopsin. These regulations will however not be further discussed here. Interested readers are referred to the FAO working documents of the Second Joint FAO/WHO/UNEP International Conference on Mycotoxins, Bangkok, 1987.

Figures 4 - 8 show that there exist significant differences among aflatoxin legislation in the various countries of the world. Sometimes one gets the impression that the framers of the regulations have taken care to be original in their work and not to pay much attention to the existing legislation of other countries. Harmonization of aflatoxin regulations would be highly desirable. Harmonization efforts should be supported by knowledge about the rationales behind the decisions that have led to the enforcement of the current regulations in the various countries of the world. The enacted regulations and those under development should be the result of sound cooperation between interested parties, drawn from industry, from the ranks of the consumers, from the scientific sector and from official circles. Only then can realistic legislation be achieved.

5. Sampling

Sampling is an integral part of the analytical procedure. The object of the sampling procedure is to obtain a laboratory sample (test portion), representative of the lot from which it is drawn. Normally, the decision whether to accept or reject a lot is based on the evidence gained from the analysis of the sample. When mycotoxins are homogeneously distributed throughout the lot to be inspected, sampling is made easy. A homogeneous distribution is encountered in the case of aflatoxin M1 in milk and milk products because of the original fluid nature of these products. This situation is exceptional. Unfortunately, most mycotoxins are heterogeneously distributed and they may occur only in a fraction of the components of the batch to be inspected. Examples are the very uneven distribution of aflatoxin B1 in a batch of peanuts (Cucullu, 1966) and some other particulate commodities, such as grain. Because the distribution of aflatoxin B1 in peanuts poses the greatest problem it has been studied rather extensively, and this example will be used further throughout this section to demonstrate the difficulties in sampling as well as the approach to come to practical sampling procedures, despite the problems.

The total error made in a test-procedure consists of three parts, namely the sampling error, the subsampling error (subsampling means that the original sample is communited, followed by sampling this ground fraction) and the analytical error. On the base of a large number of analyses Whitaker (1977) was able to calculate the contribution of each error to the total error, when a lot of peanuts, contaminated with aflatoxin B1 was sampled and analysed. As demonstrated in Figure 9 the major error component is the sampling error, whereas the subsampling and (intra laboratory) analysis error vary only slightly across all concentrations. (N.B. the inter-laboratory analytical error depends much more on the concentration).

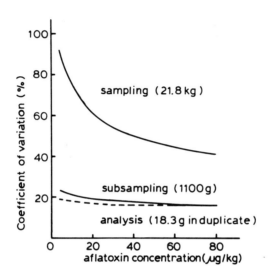

Figure 9. Relative contributions of the errors of sampling, subsampling
            and analysis to the total error (after Whitaker, 1977), courtesy
            IUPAC).

It is possible to draw a curve indicating the relationship of the probability of acceptance of a lot versus the aflatoxin concentration in the lot, given a certain tolerance. An example of such an operating characteristic (OC) curve is shown in Figure 10. (Whitaker, 1977). From Figure 10 it can be seen that the probability of accepting a lot approaches 1, when the concentration of aflatoxin approaches zero; and as the concentration becomes large, the probability of accepting approaches zero. Further, it is apparent from Figure 10 that there are two risks, the producer's risk and the consumer's risk. The producer's risk is the risk that the lot will be falsely rejected, because the aflatoxin content measured in the test portion is higher than the tolerance, although the mean concentration in the lot is below the tolerance. The consumer's risk is the risk that a lot will be falsely accepted, because the aflatoxin content measured in the test portion is lower than the tolerance, although the mean concentration in the lot exceeds the tolerance. Increasing the sample size will lead to a reduction of both the consumer's risk and the producer's risk (Figure 11) (Dickens, 1978).

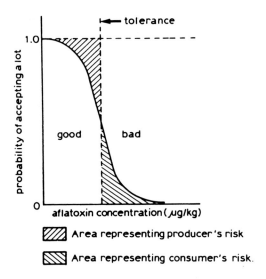

Figure 10. Relation of the probability of acceptance of a lot versus the aflatoxin concentration (operating characteristic curve) (after Whitaker, 1977, courtesy IUPAC).

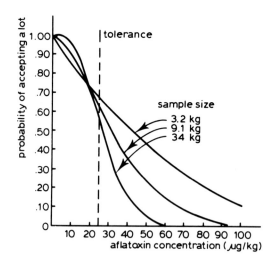

Figure 11. Effect of sample size on operating characteristic curve (after Dickens, 1978; courtesy Institut für Toxikologie, Zürich).

The ideal OC-curve is obtained when the whole lot is ground and analysed (Figure 12) (Dickens, 1978). Obviously the theoretically ideal situation has very impractical consequences: nothing would be left to sell or to buy at least not in its original form. The choice of the sample size depends on the risks that can be accepted and the costs one is willing to bear. Another possibility of influencing the producer's risk and the consumer's risk is changing the level of decision (This is a critical toxin level which has the following meaning: If the result of analysis of the test portion exceeds the limit of decision, the lot will be rejected).

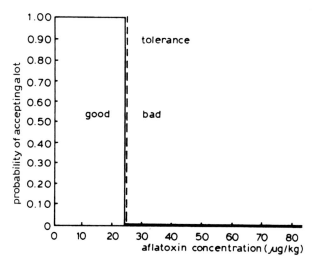

Figure 12. Ideal operating characteristic curve: the whole lot is ground and and analysed (after Dickens, 1978; courtesy Institut für Toxikologie, Zürich).

Lowering the level of decision reduces the consumer's risk, however it leads to an increase of the producer's risk (Figure 13) (Dickens, 1978). To limit these risks sampling plans have been developed in which two (or more) decision levels are used, an acceptance level and a rejection level. In such cases a lot is accepted if the outcome of the analysis of the test portion is lower than the acceptance level, rejected if it is higher than the rejection level, and reanalysed when the outcome is in between the two levels.

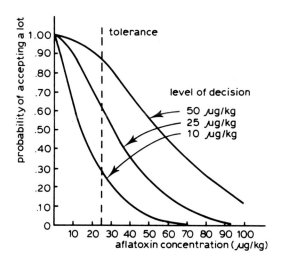

Figure 13. Effect of the level of decision on the operating characteristic curve (after Dickens, 1978; courtesy Institut für Toxikologie, Zürich).

An example of such a sampling plan is the PAC (Peanut Administrative Committee) sampling plan practised in the USA for sampling large lots of peanuts, before they are shipped to the manufacturer (Dickens, 1977). This sampling procedure involves multiple sampling and assay from representative units of 22 kg of the lot and a tolerance for the sum of the aflatoxins B1, B2, G1, and G2 of 25 mcg/kg.

Although sometimes costly, there is no doubt that very large samples of many kilogrammes of peanuts must be taken to obtain a low risk of a wrong decision for both the consumer and the producer. These large sample sizes require the samples to be subsampled to make an adequate analysis possible. Because of the possible inhomogeneity, the whole sample must be ground and homogenized. For this purpose, special instruments and techniques have been developed, such as the Dickens–Satterwhite subsampling mill (Dickens, 1969) and the Hobart vertical cuttermixer (Francis, 1979). Then, either the whole subsample is analysed or the size of the subsample is further reduced until a test portion, in size generally ranging from 20–100 g, is obtained. The compromise between solvent economy and a representative sample appears to have been set at 50 g. In the PAC testing programme for peanuts, the entire subsample (1100 g) is extracted with a mixture of 1650 ml of methanol, 1350 ml of water, 1000 ml of hexane and 22 g of sodium chloride. In addition to being costly, the solvents are an important energy resource and the used solvents are difficult to dispose of without environmental pollution. Therefore Whitaker (1980) has proposed a water slurry method which consists of extracting aflatoxins with solvent from a 130 g sample of a slurry formed by blending 1100 g of comminuted peanut kernels, 1500 ml of water and 22 g of sodium chloride in a Waring Blender. It seemed that the variance among analyses with the slurry method did not differ significantly from the variance among analyses with the official PAC procedure.

As well as the USA where the PAC sampling plan is practised, there were several other countries in 1987 which indicated having proposed or passed sampling plans for the control of mycotoxins (solely for aflatoxins) (Van Egmond, 1987). African countries with sampling plans for foods are Kenya, Malawi and Nigeria. African countries with sampling plans for feeds are Ivory Coast, Nigeria and Senegal.

It must be assumed, that the design of these sampling plans would have been based on information about the following essential factors: a critical level (control, tolerance, guideline etc. for aflatoxin); a definition of a good (acceptable) and a bad (rejectable) lot; and a statement of the acceptable or desired consumer's and producer's risks. In the absence of this information the selection of any sampling plan will be arbitrary.

6. Analytical techniques

There are two approaches possible for the detection and determination of mycotoxins: biological and chemical. Biological methods may be useful in screening for known and unknown mycotoxins. As an example, they have played a role of importance in the period of the initial discovery of the aflatoxins (Carnaghan, 1963). However, if it is known which mycotoxin(s) should be looked for, chemical assays, if available, are to be preferred, because these generally are much more specific, more rapid, more reproducible, and possess lower limits of detection. Hence, chemical assays play a role of major importance in the determination of mycotoxins. Therefore, the bioassays are briefly discussed, whereas the chemical assays are described in more detail.

Bio-assays

Generally, five categories of organisms are applied in bio-assay systems: micro-organisms, aquatic animals, terrestrial animals, organ and tissue culture systems and plants. An overview of the usefulness of these organisms for the detection of mycotoxins is given by Watson (1982).

Micro-organisms seem to be rather insensitive to mycotoxins. Burmeister (1966) surveyed over 300 species of micro-organisms for their sensitivity to aflatoxins and found only one strain of Bacillus brevis and two of Bacillus megaterium to be sensitive to aflatoxins. However, an assay method based upon the observed antibacterial action (Clements, 1968), had a high absolute limit of detection (1 μg) and was not sufficiently reproducible in collaborative studies to warrant further investigations. Other mycotoxins can inhibit the growth of micro-organisms in such a way, that useful assay procedures may be developed.

Some aquatic animals, such as brine shrimp (Artemia salina) and certain fish species (trout, zebrafish, guppy) are used in bio-assays systems to detect mycotoxins (Brown, 1968). Generally the larvae of the fish or the brine shrimps are exposed to various concentrations of toxins dissolved in aquarium water and after a certain time the percentage kill is estimated for each dilution (Waart, 1972). The brine shrimp test is one of the simplest assays, but it is relatively insensitive to mycotoxins, except some trichothecenes, sterigmatocystin and aflatoxins. A problem of the brine shrimp test may be the fact that many mycotoxins are only slightly soluble in water. The time required for the test is approximately one day and expertise is not required.

Among the terrestrial animals, ducklings and chick embryos seem to be the most sensitive to mycotoxins. In the original biological test developed during the outbreak of Turkey X Disease (Carnaghan, 1963), newly hatched ducklings were used as the test animal for determining the presence of aflatoxin isolated from suspect food, with bile duct hyperplasia as the specific measured response. The lowest dose level of 0.4 μg administered for 5 days represents the minimum intake required to induce a detectable bile duct lesion. In the chick embryo assay a small amount of extract is introduced by means of a syringe at the side of the air cell. After incubation for 3-4 weeks the number of survivors is counted. The chick embryo test appears to be one of the most sensitive bio-assay systems for mycotoxins. In addition, the test is reproducible and especially useful for aflatoxin B1 assay, as typical lesions are observed in the embryo with subacute levels of aflatoxin B1, less that 0.1 μg/egg. The chick embryo test has been studied collaboratively with success (Verret, 1973) and the method has been adopted as the official final action method by the Association of Official Analytical Chemists (AOAC, 1984). The long incubation period makes the chick embryo test one of the slower bio-assays, which is the major disadvantage. When screening for trichothecenes, a group of mycotoxins exhibiting dermatitic activity, the laboratory animal skin test has proven to be useful (Chung, 1974). Extracts of suspected commodities and cultures are applied on the shaved skin of a rabbit or a rat and the skin is inspected for some days. Responses as erythema, edema and necrosis indicate the presence of trichothecenes in the extract. The method is reliable and has an absolute limit of detection of ca. 0.01 μg/test.

The advantage of using cell cultures to detect mycotoxins is that low concentrations can give a perceptible response. Cultures of liver, kidney and muscle cells may serve as test material. This in-vitro assay is carried out by adding extracts of suspect commodities or fungal cultures to the culture medium. Cultivation is continued for several days and the degree of cytotoxicity as well as cytogenetic effects and morphological changes are noted at certain time intervals (Umeda, 1977). Exposure of rat liver cells to concentrations of 0.1 μg aflatoxin b1/ml medium leads to marked damage (Umeda, 1971). A limitation of the cell culture method is the fact that many media used for culturing fungi appear to be toxic and therefore they may not serve as a control.

The last category to be mentioned are the plants. The phytotoxicity assays are based on the ability of some mycotoxins to inhibit the growth and germination of seeds of higher plants. Schoental (1965) found that water suspensions of aflatoxins with a concentration of 25 μg/ml added to agar plates containing watercress seeds led to complete inhibition of seed germination, whereas chlorophyll deficiency in the seedling ("albinism") was found at concentrations of 1-2.5 μg/ml. Burmeister (1970) reported that 0.5 μg of T-2 toxin inhibited the germination of pea seed by 50% when the seeds were soaked overnight in the solution.

Bio-assays may be useful when there is no chemical assay available. Bio-assays have proved of primary use in screening for mycotoxins. However, their use in the surveillance of food and feedstuffs is of minor importance as they generally lack specificity, reproducibility and rapidity.

Chemical assays

The limitation of bio-assay techniques to detect and determine mycotoxins led chemists to develop more selective and reliable methods of analysis. Generally all chemical analytical methods for the detection and determination of mycotoxins contain the basic steps as outlined in Figure 14. The problems in sampling have already been discussed. Homogenized test portions that are taken for analysis usually vary in weight from ca. 20-100 g, a range resulting from a compromise between homogeneity requirements and practical requirements.

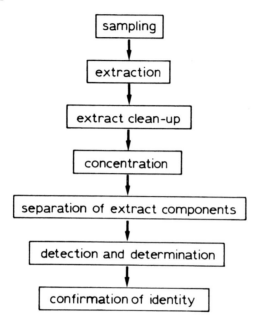

Figure 14. Analytical procedure for mycotoxin determination

Extraction

The first step in chemical analysis involves extraction of the test portion to separate the component of interest from the bulk of the matrix components and to obtain the materials of interest in a manageable form. Generally, mycotoxins are extracted with organic solvents such as chloroform, dichloromethane, acetonitrile, ethylacetate, acetone and methanol. Contact between solvent and solid substrate is accomplished either for a short period (1-3 min) in a high speed blender, or for a longer period (30 min) by shaking in a flask. Liquids may be extracted in a separatory funnel or absorbed to a hydrophylic matrix which is (pre-) packed in a column, after which extraction is accomplished by eluting the column with an extraction solvent. An example of the latter extraction technique is the procedure to determine aflatoxin M1 in milk in which a laboratory-prepared Celite column is used (Schuller, 1973).

The choice of the solvent depends on the chemical properties of the toxin to be extracted as well as on the properties of the matrix. Often, mixtures of solvents or solvents with small amounts of water and acids, are found to be most efficient. While the solubility of many mycotoxins in water is low, aqueous solvents may penetrate hydrophilic tissues, leading to a most efficient extraction by the non-aqueous solvents. Two of the best-known and practiced methods of analysis for aflatoxins, the CB (Contaminants Branch)-method (Eppley, 1966) and the EC (European Community)-method (Commission of the European Communities, 1976), employ a mixture of chloroform and water to extract aflatoxins.

Clean-up

Since mycotoxins are normally only present at very low levels, a strong concentration of the extract is necessary to make detection possible. The frequent presence of lipids and other substances that may interfere in the final detection makes it necessary to clean-up the extract prior to concentration, by column clean-up, liquid-liquid extraction, and/or co-precipitation of impurities. Several column chromatographic clean-up steps are possible with materials such as silica gel, modified silica gel, aluminium ozyde, polyamide Florisil[R] and Sephadex[R]. Silica gel is most frequently used. Columns can be packed in the laboratory. However, pre-packed columns are now commercially obtainable, in rather many recently published analytical methods for mycotoxins these columns are used. The advantges of such pre-packed columns e.g. SEP-pak[R], Baker[R] are obvious. Variations in preparation of columns between analysts are eliminated whereas time, needed to prepare the columns is saved. On the other hand, variations between lots of prepacked columns have been reported, (Scott, 1984) and they do offer the possibility of easily introducing slight variations in the column composition (for instance adjustment of the water content or column size). The sample extract is usually added to the column in an appropriate solvent, after which the column is washed with one or more solvents in which the toxins are insoluble or less soluble than the impurities. Then the solvent composition is changed in such a way that the toxins are selectively eluted from the column. The eluate is collected and concentrated.

Liquid-liquid extraction may also be carried out in separating funnels, for instance pentane against methanol-water. Since most mycotoxins are not lipophylic, fats can be removed in this way without loss of toxin. In some analytical procedures, precipitating reagents are used. Examples are lead acetate and fresh ferric hydroxide gel to precipitate gossypol pigments in extract of cottonseed (Pons, 1965) (Wiseman, 1967), cupric carbonate to remove chlorophyll (Velasco, 1970) and silver nitrate to remove alkaloids from cocoa extracts (Scott, 1969).

The above mentioned clean-up techniques are in fact separation procedures in which groups of substances with certain physicochemical properties can be separated from one another. In this way the greater part of the co-extracted material can be removed. The choice of the clean-up procedure may depend on the method used for detection and determination, the required limit of detection, the speed of analysis and the recovery.

Extracts that have been cleaned-up are usually concentrated by evaporatating the solvent in a rotary evaporator under reduced pressure, or by using a steam bath, while keeping the extract under a stream of nitrogen. The residue is redissolved in a small volume of solvent, quantitatively transferred to a small vial and brought to a specified volume. Depending on the toxin and the ultimate separation and detection step to be used, derivatization of the mycotoxin of interest may be necessary to make it measurable or to optimalize its chromatographic behaviour.

Ultimate separation, detection and determination

Despite extraction and clean-up, the final extract may contain large amounts of other co-extracted substances possibly interfering with mycotoxin determination. Several possibilities exist to separate the mycotoxins from the matrix to allow qualitative and quantitative determination. Chromatographic procedures, which are based on physical separation principles, are most often applied. They are used in combination with visual or instrumental determination of the mycotoxin(s) of interest. Immunochemical procedures, which are based on complex biochemical binding and selection principles are rapidly gaining ground however in mycotoxin research.

Chromatographic procedures

Chromatographic processes involve solute partitioning between two phases, a stationary phase (the chromatographic bed) and a mobile phase (liquid or gas), carrying substances to be separated through the chromatographic bed. The stationary phase retards more or less the progress of substances through the bed, depending on their physicochemical properties, so that a separation into components can be achieved. For mycotoxin assays the following types of chromatography can be distinguished:

- open column chromatography
- thin layer chromatography
- high performance liquid chromatography
- gas liquid chromatography

a. Open column chromatography

Open column chromatography has been mentioned already as a technique often used in clean-up procedures. A special design - the glass minicolumn with an internal diameter of ca. 5 mm - can be used for the detection of some mycotoxins in certain commodities. In the test procedure according to Rome (1975) the minicolumn is packed with successive zone of adsorbents such as alumina, silica gel and Florisil^R with calcium sulphate drier at both ends and held in place with glass wool (Fig. 15). A chloroform extract is applied on the top of the column, and drained by gravity. Then, descending chromatography with a mixture of chloroform and acetone is applied, trapping the aflatoxins as a tight band at the top of the Florisil^R layer, where they can be detected by their blue fluorescence under U.V. light (Fig. 16). By comparing a sample column with a column containing a known amount of aflatoxins, it is possible to judge whether the sample contains more or less aflatoxins than the standard. Contrary to thin layer chromatographic techniques, the minicolumn method of Romer (1975) does not distinguish between the different aflatoxins. The method of Romer (1975) was subjected to a successful collaborative study (Rome, 1976) and has been adopted by the AOAC as an official first action method for the detection of aflatoxins in almonds, white and yellow maize, peanut and cotton seed meals, peanuts, peanut butter, pistachio nuts and mixed feeds (AOAC, 1984). As well as for the aflatoxins, similar minicolumn procedures have been developed for some other mycotoxins that flouresce when irradiated with U.V. light, such as ochratoxin A (see figure 1) in a wide range of products (Holaday, 1976) and zearalenone (see figure 1) in maize, wheat and sorghum (Holaday, 1980). The limits of detection achieved vary from ca. 5-15 μg/kg for zearalenone.

Minicolumn methods are "go-no go" methods, which require little time and no sophisticated equipment. This makes them useful for field screening tests by scientists and technicians in developing countries. Therefore the Organization for Economic Cooperation and Development (OECD) has published some selected minicolumn procedures for aflatoxins in a Handbook on rapid detection of mycotoxins (OECD, 1982). Although having some advantages, minicolumn methods have certain limitations: The interpretation of the picture on the column requires some experience and it may be especially difficult, when "dirty" extracts, containing flourescent compounds other than the toxin of interest are applied to the column. In those cases, false positives results may occur. Minicolumn methods are at best semi-quantitative and generally have a higher limit of detection and less sensitivity, separation power and selectivity than is obtained by using thin layer chromatographic and high performance liquid chromatographic procedures. It may be expected that enzyme immuno assay will supersede minicolumn methods for rapid screening purposes.

b. Thin layer chromatography

In thin layer chromatography (TLC) the stationary phase consists of a thin layer of adsorbent particles bound on a plate and the mobile phase flows through this layer through capillary forces. In the first years of mycotoxin research thin layer chromatography (TLC) became a very common and popular technique to separate extract components and nowadays there are still numerous applications. Initially separations were carried out in one dimension using a single developing solvent. Later two-dimensional TLC was introduced to mycotoxin research (Kiermeier, 1970). It is a powerful separation technique in which a second development is carried out in a direction at right angles to the first one, using a different developing solvent. This provides a much better separation than one-dimensional TLC and is required especially in those cases where low levels have to be detected, e.g. Aflatoxin M1, in milk, and if extracts contain many interfering substances e.g. feedstuffs and roasted peanuts.

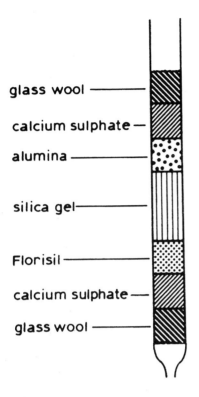

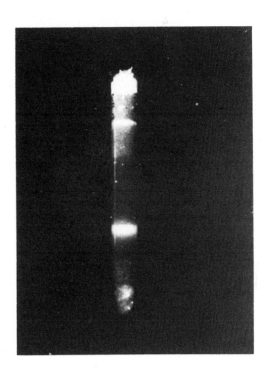

Figure 15. Packing of a mini–column according to Romer (1975).

Figure 16. Adsorption of aflatoxin B_1 to the Florisil^R layer of a mini–column.

In thin layer chromatography a wide range of adsorbents can be used. For mycotoxin research silica gel TLC plates are most often used as this type of adsorbent generally offers the best possibility of separating the toxin of interest from matrix components. Both pre–coated and self–coated plates can be used. Self–coated plates allow a free selection of adsorbents and a free selection of additives. Calcium sulphate can be added as a binder of the silica gel to the glass plate. EDTA has been used by Stubblefield (1979 B) as a complexing agent for contaminants in the silica gel to prevent streaking of citrinin spots. Pre–coated plates, on the other hand are ready to use and they generally possess more uniform and rigid layer and do permit a certain choice of support, e.g. glass, plastic or aluminium. The characteristics of pre–coated as well as self–coated plates may differ from brand to brand and sometimes even from batch to batch, leading to different separation behaviour, as can be seen in Figure 17, where a mixture of aflatoxins B1, B2, G1, and G2 has been separated on three different types of plates, after which the plates are viewed under U.V. light. (These four main aflatoxins have been named according to their colour of fluorescence (blue or green) and their relative mobility on the TLC plate (RF value).

Thin layer plates can be used in different formats. Most separation problems may be resolved using a square 20x20 cm plate; however the use of 10x10 cm plates and even 7x7 cm self–cut plates will often lead to good results as well. Especially for two–dimensional separation procedures, the use of the smaller sizes saves much time. Examples of analytical procedures in which two–dimensional separations are carried out on small TLC plates are the multi–mycotoxin method of Patterson (1979), the methods of Van Egmond (1980) for the determination of sterigmatocystin in cheese, the method of Stubblefield (1981) for the determination of aflatoxins in animal tissue and the method of

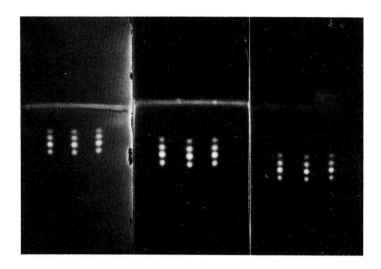

Figure 17. Separation of a mixture of aflatoxin standards
on several types of SiO$_2$ TLC plates.

Paulsch (1982) for the determination of ochratoxin A in pig kidneys. The smaller plate sizes additionally offer the possibility of developing the plates not only in especially designed developing chambers, but also in simple beakers, which is attractive to laboratories with limited supply of glassware. They may also be used in series of 10 at a time in a so-called multiplate rack (figure 18), thus significantly reducing the overall time required for a series of TLC runs.

In the TLC determination of mycotoxins generally 5-15 μl of extract is applied to the plate. Depending on the desired accuracy and precision, different types of applicators are used. For screening purposes the disposable qualitative capillary pipettes or precision syringes, which are more accurate and precise, are used. Moreover, the latter allow the intermittant application of larger volumes under inert atmosphere by using them in combination with a repeating dispensor eventually incorporated in a spotting device. The spotting of sample and standard(s) is normally carried out according to a spotting pattern, prescribed as a part of the whole analytical procedure. Different spotting patterns apply to one-dimensional TLC, or, in the case of "dirty" extracts, two-dimensional TLC. In two-dimensional TLC the sample extract is spotted at a corner of the TLC plate and two developments are carried out successively parallel to the two sides of the plate using two different developing solvents. The two solvents must be compatible and independent, i.e. there should be little correlation between the retention patterns in both systems, otherwise the spots tend to agglomerate along the bisector of the plate.

An example of the use of two-dimensional TLC is the procedure used in the official EEC-method for the determination of aflatoxin B1 in animal feedstuffs (Commission of the European Communities, 1976) (Figure 19): An aliquot of extract is spotted at A and known amounts of aflatoxin B1 standard are spotted at B. The plate is then developed in the first direction with a mixture of diethyl ether, methanol and water (94+4.5+1.5) and, after drying, the plate is turned 90° and developed in the second direction with a mixture of chloroform and acetone (9+1). Detection and quantification is carried out under longwave U.V. light (365 nm). In Figure 20 the result of a two-dimensional TLC separation of an extract of peanut butter contaminated with aflatoxin B1 is shown. With the help of the co-developed B1 standards, the well-separated B1 spot from the sample can be located. By means of a densitometer the intensities of fluorescence of the B1 spot from sample and

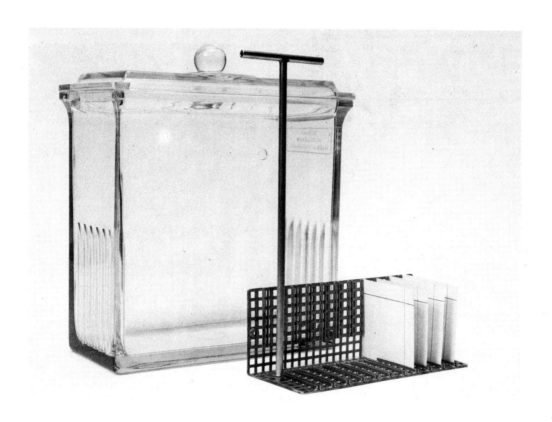

Figure 18. Stainless steel rack for parallel chromatography
of ten 6.7x6.7 cm TLC plates.

standard can be compared and thus the B1 concentration in the initial sample can be calculated.

If a densitometer is not available which will often be the case in developing countries, an anti-diagonal spotting pattern may be used as originally developed by Beljaars (1973) for the determination of aflatoxin B1 in peanuts (Figure 21): An aliquot of sample extract is spotted at A and different amounts of B1 standard are spotted at the points B. The plate is developed two-dimensionally, and detection and quantification are again carried out under U.V. light (Figure 22). With the help of the row of two-dimensionally developed B1 standards, B1 from the extract can be located and its concentration estimated by comparing its intensity of flourescence with that of the different B1 standards. As all the B1 spots are in a line and rather close to each other, such an estimation is easier than visual comparison with standard spots developed in the side lanes, as in the case in the densitometric spotting pattern. However the technique is only applicable if the standard spots appear on a "free" part of the plate after two-dimensional development.

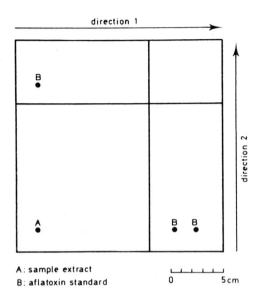

direction 1

direction 2

B
•

A
•

B B
• •

A: sample extract
B: aflatoxin standard

0   5 cm

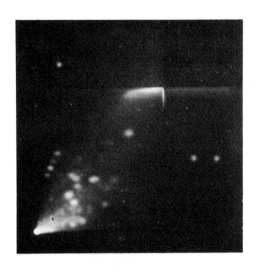

Figure 19. Scheme of the spotting pattern for two-dimensional TLC (densitometric quantification).

Figure 20. Separation of an extract of peanut butter submitted to two-dimensional TLC, using the densitometric spotting pattern.

Two dimensional TLC procedures have also been developed for the determination of other mycotoxins such as for zearalenone (Jemmali, 1977), sterigmatocystin (van Egmond, 1980), and ochratoxin A (Paulsch, 1982) (Figure 1) and in a multi-mycotoxin method (Patterson, 1979).

The fortunate characteristic that aflatoxins emit the energy of absorbed longwave U.V. light as fluorescence light, enables the analyst to detect these compounds at low levels. Unfortunately not all mycotoxins can be detected by such a simple method. Many do not fluoresce under U.V. light, some show U.V. or visible light absorption, while others do not. If the latter is the case, sometimes the mycotoxin can be made visible by spraying a reagent on the plate or by exposing the plate to reagent vapour. An example of such derivatization is the spraying technique used for the visualization of sterigmatocystin, a toxin sometimes occurring in grains (Scott) and in cheese (Northolt, 1980). Stack (1971) has found that spraying with an AlCl3-solution leads to an Al-complex with the keto- and hydroxyl groups of the sterigmatocystin molecule (Figure 1) resulting in an enhancement of the fluorescence intensity of ca. 100 times. In addition, the colour of fluorescence changes from brick-red to yellow. Another application of AlCl3 reagent is included in the procedure for the determination of deoxynivalenol (DON) (Figure 1), where use is made of AlCl3 impregnated silica gel plates (Trucksess, 1984). After heating the developed TLC plate, DON appears as a blue fluorescent spot under longwave U.V. light.

In spite of all the clean-up techniques used, there are still substances which behave in the same manner during TLC separation as the mycotoxin being determined. In order to minimize the risk of false-positives, the identity of the mycotoxin in positive samples should be confirmed especially when the analyst is not experienced in mycotoxin assays. The most reliable method for this purpose is high resolution mass spectrometry (HRMS). HMRS in combination with TLC however is rather time-consuming and most laboratories in the developing countries will not be equipped with this sophisticated type of apparatus. Therefore more simple techniques have to be applied. Probably the simplest

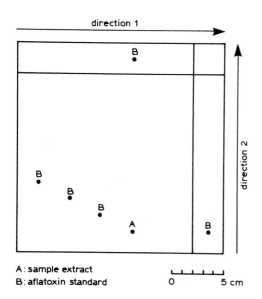

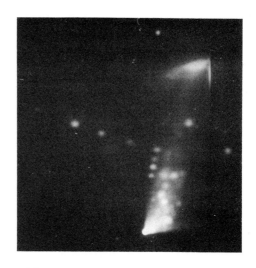

Figure 21. Scheme of the anti-diagonal spotting pattern for two-dimensional TLC (visual quantification).

Figure 22. Separation of an extract of peanut butter submitted to two-dimensional TLC, using TLC, using the anti-diagonal spotting pattern.

ways of confirming the presence of mycotoxins are the use of additional solvent systems or the application of supplementary chromatography, by repeating the TLC procedure now with an internal standard, superimposed on the extract spot before developing the plate. After completion of TLC this superimposed standard and the "presumed" toxin spot from the sample must coincide. Another possibility is to spray the developed TLC plate with a reagent, so that the colour (of fluorescence) of the mycotoxin spot changes. An example of the latter possibility is the spraying test with a dilute solution of sulphuric acid (Smith, 1962), which leads to a change in the colour of flourescence of aflatoxin spots from blue to yellow. Although the above described tests, if negative, would rule out the presence of the mycotoxin concerned, they do not provide positive confirmatory evidence.

Positive identification can be obtained by formation of specific derivatives with altered chromatograhic properties. Both mycotoxin standard and suspected sample are submitted to the same derivatization reaction. Consequently, in positive samples a derivative from the mycotoxin should appear, identical to the derivative from the mycotoxin standard. Confirmatory reactions may be carried out in test tubes, or, preferably, directly on a TLC plate, thus using the separation power of TLC. An example of the latter technique is the confirmation procedure adopted in the official EC-method for the determination of aflatoxin in animal feedstuffs and originally published by Verhülsdonk (1977). In this procedure a so-called separation-reaction-separation procedure is carried out (Figure 23). Hydrochloric acid is sprayed after the first separation run, the reaction takes place. Then a second separation is carried out in second direction, under identical conditions, after which the isolate blue fluorescent spot of aflatoxin B2a, a "water adduct" of Aflatoxin B1, is visible, which can be recognized with the help of a B1 standard, spotted on the same plate, which has undergone the same procedure. Other (unreacted) components lie on a diagonal line, bisecting the plate, as the separation was carried out in both directions under exactly identical conditions. In Figure 24 the result of such a confirmatory test applied to feedstuff contaminated with aflatoxins B1 and G1 is shown.

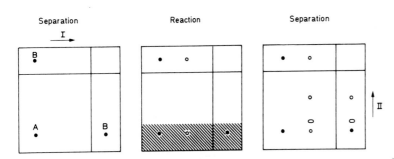

Separation   Reaction   Separation

A: spotting place sample   ▨ area to be   ○ specific reactionproduct
B: spotting place standard   sprayed

Figure 23. Schematic representation of the two-dimensional confirmatory test of Verhülsdonk (1977).

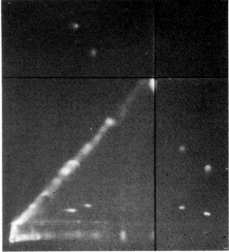

Figure 24. Result of the confirmatory test of Verhülsdonk (1977), applied to rabbit feedstuff.

The described techniques for confirmation of aflatoxin B1 are also applicable to aflatoxin G1 however not to aflatoxins B2 and G2 of which the terminal furan ring is saturated. An in situ confimatory test has also been developed for aflatoxin M1 by Trucksess (1976). In this procedure a reaction is carried out between trifluoroacetic acid and aflatoxin M1 on the origin spot of a TLC plate before development of the plate.

In situ derivatization procedures on TLC plates followed by TLC of the reaction product(s) to establish the identity of mycotoxins other than aflatoxins are rather scarce. Van Egmond (1980) described a test for the confirmation of identity of sterigmatocystin (see Figure 1) in a cheese extract. In the test which is based on the principles of the separation-reaction-separation procedure (see Figure 23) a mixture of trifluoroacetic acid and benzene is sprayed on the TLC plate and after the reaction and a second development the reaction product is visualized with AlCl3 spray reagent (Stack, 1971). Paulsch (1982) developed a confirmatory test for ochratoxin A (see figure 1) in pig kidneys, based on the findings of Kleinau (1981). Ochratoxin A spots separated after two-dimensional TLC are esterified on the TLC plate with methanol-H2SO4 after which the plate is developed for the third time. The methyl ester of ochratoxin A is visible under long wave U.V. light as a flourescent spot with an Rf value higher than that of ochratoxin A. Like ochratoxin A, the methyl ester undergoes the same change in colour of flourescence from green to blue when the pH of the plate is changed from acid to alkaline by exposing the plate to the vapour of ammonia and this phenomenon can be considered as an additional confirmation of identity.

The use of thin layer chromatography as a technique to separate mycotoxins from matrix components has decreased in recent years in favour of high performance liquid chromatography and to a lesser extent of gas liquid chromatography (especially for the determination of trichothecenes). A further decrease will probably occur in the near future in favour of the immunoassays, especially enzyme-linked immunosorbent assay. Nevertheless thin layer chromatography is a reliable, relatively simple and still a frequently used technique for the determination of mycotoxins. Especially its two dimensional application which offers a good resolution, and consequently low limits of detection. Special advantages of thin layer chromatography are the possibility of carrying out in situ derivatization procedures to confirm the presence of mycotoxins, the ability to store plates for latter interpretation and the fact that the analyst has a certain "contact" with the result of the separation, because the human eye itself can act as a detector. Thin layer chromatography is particularly recommended to those, inexperienced in the analysis of food and feed for mycotoxins and who cannot afford to purchase sophisticated instrumentation.

c. High performance liquid chromatography

In High Performance Liquid Chromatography (HPLC), adsorbent particles are densely packed in a tube (column), and the mobile phase is pumped through the column under high pressure. HPLC became available for the analysis of foodstuffs in the early seventies and probably the first published application for mycotoxin research dates from 1973 (Seiber, 1973). After a somewhat hesitating start, the technique became of rapidly growing importance in the determination of mycotoxins, particularly when several types of column packings and (fluorescence-) detectors became available. The introduction of autosamplers and computerized data retrieval systems made HPLC in principle very useful for large scale analyses.

In the first applications which concerned aflatoxin assays, SiO2 columns were used in combination with chloroform -or dichloro methane- containing mobile phases, and detection was by means of U.V. detectors (λ=254 nm or 365 nm) (Seiber, 1973) (Pons, 1976) (Kmieciak, 1976). U.V. detection however is not very selective, whereas the obtained limits of detection for aflatoxins are relatively high (in the order of ca. 1-2 ng of each aflatoxin (Pons, 1976) or expressed as a relative detection limit, ca. 50 μg afltoxins B1/kg for groundnuts (Kmieciak, 1976). Therefore the use of U.V. detectors for aflatoxin assay has been largely discontinued, when the more selective fluorescence detectors became available. Initially the fluorescence detectors had limitations in detectability as well, because aflatoxins B1 and B2 do not exhibit strong fluorescence in normal phase solvents and B1 and G1 do not exhibit strong fluorescence in reverse phase solvents. Consequently the limits of detection of the mentioned aflatoxins could not compete with those obtained in thin layer chromatography. Several efforts have been undertaken to improve the intensity of fluorescence of the aflatoxins, which resulted in four main techniques:

1) In the procedures of Takahashi (1977) and Haghighi (1981), the sample and standard solutions are treated with acid (i.e. trifluoroacetic acid) to convert aflatoxins B1 and G1 to the respective hemiacetals, B2a and G2a. The hemiacetals fluoresce as strongly as B2 and G2 in reverse phase solvents. A disadvantage of the technique is, that it involves an extra step needed for the chemical conversion. In addition, it may be questionable, whether conversion always occurs quantitatively.

2) Panalaks (1977) and Zimmerli (1977) introduced the use of silica gel packed flowcells for fluorimetric detection of aflatoxins in normal phase solvents. In the adsorbed state, the aflatoxins B1 and B2 fluoresce much more intensively than they do in solution. The limits of detection thus obtained are in the same order of magnitude as those based upon TLC with fluorescence detection. The life expectancy of the packed flow cell may vary depending on the number and state of the samples that are injected. In practice, contamination of the flow cell occurs, caused by deposits from dirty extracts accumulating on the silica gel over a period of time thus necessitating frequent changes. The latter is a restriction of the practical use of a packed flow cell, especially when the detector has no easily accessible flow cell. Panalaks (1977) indicated that it was convenient to regenerate the flow cell by pumping through a more polar solvent because this caused a change in transparency of the silica gel.

3) Manabe (1978) introduced a new mobile phase which prevented the usual quenching of aflatoxins B1 and B2. A solvent consisting of a mixture of toluene, ethyl acetate,

formic acid and methanol would lead to a minimum detectable amount of aflatoxin B1 of ca. 0.3 ng, whereas application of the method to food and feed revealed that levels of 10–20 µg/kg of the four aflatoxins B1, B2, G1 and G2, were still detectable. Compared to the other techniques used to enhance the fluorescence of aflatoxins B1 and B2, the limits of detection claimed by Manabe (1978) are not too impressive, however the technique is the easiest to apply. A disadvantage is the possible decomposition of aflatoxins B1 and G1 on the column due to the presence of acid in the mobile phase. Care should be taken not to use too high amounts of acid and to check with standards, whether any decomposition occurs under the optimal separation conditions.

4) Treatment of aflatoxins B1 and G1 with iodine to produce more intensely fluorescing derivatives has been reported by Davis (1979). The finding was made applicable to reverse phase HPLC by Davis (1980) and the application has been further refined by Thorpe (1982) who described the post-column derivatization to the detection of aflatoxins by reverse phase HPLC. The iodine addition enhances the fluorescence of aflatoxins B1 and G1 approximately 50 fold without affecting the fluorescence of aflatoxins B2 and G2. An advantage of this procedure is that the derivative is formed from an already separated aflatoxin peak, which means that the reaction conditions for sample and standard are the same and the occurrence of multiple reaction products is not important as long as the reaction is repeatable. Additional advantages are the need to derivatize only the portion of the sample to be injected into the liquid chromatograph and the ability to make sequential injections into the liquid chromatograph with and without post-column reagent addition, which confirms the presence or absence of aflatoxins B1 and G1. The procedure has proven to be successful for the analysis of samples of maize and peanut butter (contaminated at levels ranging from 0.5–2.0 µg/kg) and also methods have been developed which allow the determination of aflatoxins in citrus-containing mixed feedstuffs at a level of ca. 1 µg/kg (Tuinstra, 1983), (van Egmond, 1987B). Citrus pulp is a popular ingredient in feedstuffs in Europe and known to lead to strong interferences in many TLC and HPLC procedures. Therefore the method of van Egmond (1987B) is currently being considered for an EC-collaborative study with the aim of adopting it as an official method of the European Communities. Figure 25 presents a reverse phase HPLC chromatogram as obtained from an extract of feeding stuff containing citrus pulp, prepared according to this method.

HPLC methods have also become available for the analysis of milk and milk products for aflatoxin M1 (see Fig. 1). Most of these methods use reverse phase HPLC, which does not lead to problems in detectability. AFlatoxin M1 fluoresces much more intensively in reverse phase solvents than aflatoxin B1, so that no special provisions of derivatizations are necessary. The limits of detection obtained are comparable with those obtained in (two-dimensional) thin layer chromatography and some of these methods are widely used already in surveillance and monitoring programmes. An example of an excellent HPLC separation of an extract of milk powder, prepared according to the method of Stubblefield (1979A), is shown in Figure 26. In addition to the aflatoxins, HPLC separation procedures have been developed for other mycotoxins. In most of these procedures U.V. detection is applied, however for various mycotoxins (i.e. ochratoxin A, zearalenone, some ergot alkaloids, and some Alternaria toxins) fluorescence detectors have shown to be useful. It is inappropriate to review here all existing procedures that have been published and interested persons are referred to a comprehensive review, with many technical details, prepared by Scott (1981)

High performance liquid chromatography has partly superseded thin layer chromatography in the analysis of food for mycotoxins. The reasons for this development are obvious. Separations can be accomplished in a matter of minutes, HPLC methods generally provide good quantitative information and the equipment employed in HPLC systems can be automated rather easily, which makes the technique attractive to routine and quality control laboratories.

HPLC has limitations as well. Although resolutions are much better than those obtained using one-dimensional TLC the use of two-dimensional chromatography in HPLC is hardly possible. It is just the latter technique that has proven to be such a powerful separation tool when applied to thin layer chromatography, especially when low limits of detection are required for "dirty" sample extracts. The cost of equipment for thin layer

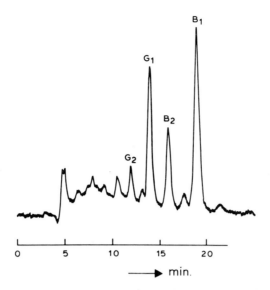

Figure 25. C_{18} reverse phase HPLC chromatogram of an extract
of feedstuff containing citruspulp, contaminated
with aflatoxins B_1, B_2, G_1 and G_2 at ca. 12, 3, 8,
and 1 µg/kg respectively, prepared according to
van Egmond (1987).

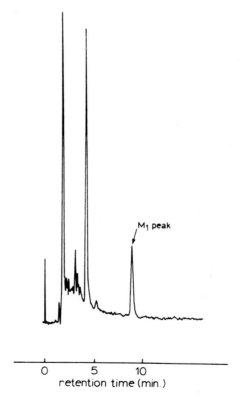

Figure 26. C_{18} reverse phase HPLC chromatogram of an extract of
milk powder, containing ca. 0.4 µg M_1/kg, prepared
according to Stubblefield (1979, courtesy Dr Mulders,
the Netherlands).

chromatography (except densitometers), is relatively cheap compared with the expensive instrumentation for HPLC. The extensive experience required to obtain the maximum benefit from an HPLC system constitutes another limitation, whereas TLC can be learned relatively easily. The few published studies in which HPLC has been compared with TLC for the determination of aflatoxins in peanuts (Crosby, 1978) and, corn and peanuts (de Vries, 1982) have indicated that both techniques provide results that agree rather well. In the developing countries, the simplicity and low cost of thin layer chromatography should not be given up lightly for the more glamorous HPLC. One should bear in mind that sophisticated systems are weak if the availability of supplies, spare ports and service form a problem, as may be the case in many of the developing countries, and HPLC should not be the first choice there, when setting up a system for monitoring and surveying agricultural commodities for mycotoxins. Care should be taken not to choose haphazardly a sophisticated technique for sophistications sake!

d. Gas chromatography

In gas chromatography (GC), the mobile phase is a carrier gas, led through a column, containing a solid adsorbent or a liquid stationary phase. The use of GC in the mycotoxin analysis has been limited, as most of the mycotoxins are not volatile and must therefore be derivatized before they can be gas chromatographed. In addition, the fact that many of the mycotoxins are readily detected and determined at low levels of concentration using TLC and HPLC techniques, as discussed in the foregoing paragraphs, has not stimulated the development of gas chromatographic assays.

Although some gas chromatographic methods have become available in the 1970s for the detection and determination of patulin (see Figure 1) in apple juice (Pohland, 1970), penicillic acid in maize and in rice (Pero, 1972) and zearalenone in maize (Mirocha, 1974), the only significant advantage over TLC and HPLC techniques is the potential use of mass spectrometers as highly selective and sensitive detectors. However, this situation is quite different for one important group of the mycotoxins, to which belong T-2 toxin and deoxynivalenol, the trichothecenes (see Figure 1). Chemical determination of the trichothecenes by TLC and HPLC is difficult due to the fact that these compounds have no fluorescent properties, nor do trichothecenes absorb appreciably in the ultraviolet range. Although TLC methods have been developed using visualization reagents, the obtained detection limits are relatively high compared to GC. GC permits the detection and quantitation of most of the more common trichothecenes. Trichothecenes can be gas chromatographed as their trimethylsilyl- (TMS) or heptafluorobutyryl- (HFB) derivatives, whereas detection relies upon flame ionization detectors (FID) and electron capture detectors (ECD). Because the trichothecenes are of minor importance in developing countries, the GC techniques to determine them will not be further discussed here. The possibilities for employing GC in combination with mass spectrometers for quantitative assays of commodities for mycotoxins will not be discussed either. The practical use of these sophisticated systems is limited to those laboratories who can afford to purchase these expensive computer-controlled systems.

Immunochemical procedures

Immunochemical procedures are based upon quite different principles than chromatographic procedures. Immunochemical procedures involve reversible binding between antigens (=the analyte e.g. the mycotoxin of interest) and selective antibodies, leading to a specific antigen-antibody complex. The production of antibodies can be evoked by immunizing test animals with an immunogen. An antiserum may then be obtained from the blood. Sometimes the immunogen is identical to the antigen, e.g. for proteins or polypeptides with a molecular weight >5000 Dalton. Mycotoxins generally have molecular weights too low to directly evoke antibodies, when administered to animals. These so-called haptens have to be covalently conjugated with proteins before immunization can occur. The antibodies (antiserum) are a group of serum proteins also referred to as immunoglobulins. Most of the immunoglobulins belong to the IgG class. Because these immunoglobulins possess not only antibody reaction sites but also antigenic determinant sites, the immunoglobulins themselves can serve as antigens when injected into a foreign animal. This possibility is applied in some types of immunoassays. (e.g. Inhibition-type Enzyme-linked Immunosorbent Assay, discussed later in this paragraph). It goes beyond the scope of this chapter to discuss the details of hapten conjugation and production of antibodies against mycotoxins. More important to know is that antisera against some of the mycotoxins (aflatoxins in particular) have been produced (Chu, 1983). Some of these are now commercially available, although often as part of a test kit only.

Classical immuno-analytical techniques are based on the interaction (in solution) between native antigens and specific antibodies, leading to precipitation of the antigen complex. This precipitation is a measure of the antigen or antibody concentration and is suitable for measuring antigen-concentrations (in solution) of the order of μg-mg/ml. When the antigen is present in low concentrations, as is usually the case with mycotoxins, labelled antigen has to be used in competition to measure the complex formation indirectly. The label can be an enzyme, a radio-isotope or some other marker which can be detected and quantified. For the determination of mycotoxins, the use of immunoassays has been limited to date (1987) to Enzyme Immuno Assay (EIA) and Radio Immuno Assay (RIA).

a. Enzyme Immuno Assay

In the performance of Enzyme Immuno Assay the reversible binding between antigen and antibody plays a central role, as is the case with all immunochemical procedures. The formation of the antigen-antibody complex can be measured indirectly by using enzyme-labelled antigen in competition. The quantity of enzyme is a measure for the amount of antigen-antibody complex. It can be measured with chromogenic substrate. At present, most Enzyme Immuno Assays for the determination of mycotoxins are of the type: Enzyme Linked Immunosorbent Assay (ELISA). In ELISA either the antibody or the (conjugated) antigen is immobilized on a solid support. Often microtitreplates or microtitrestrips are used as solid support. These are transparent plates (strips of polystyrene or polyvinylchloride with 96 small wells (in the case of strips: 8 or 12 wells) (see Figure 27). Microtitre plates and strips have several advantages above separate tubes. They are easier to handle, they can be washed and read out rather easily, and they are suitable for large series of analyses. The wells of microtitreplates (strips) can be rather uniformly and reproducibly coated with antibody or protein-conjugated antigen. This coating can be realized by bringing a solution with antibody or conjugated antigen in the wells for a period varying from a few hours to one day. The solution is poured out of the wells after coating and the solid phase is washed a few times. Dry, coated plates can be kept in stock. Usually factory-coated plates and strips are supplied, as parts of commercial ELISA-kits.

At the time of writing (1987) mycotoxin-ELISA's have been published not only for aflatoxin B1 (Biermann 1980A, 1980B), (Pestka, 1981), (Neogen Corporation, 1986) but also for aflatoxins M1 (Harder, 1979), (Frémy, 1984), (Jackman, 1985), (Märtlbauer, 1985); ochratoxin A (Morgan, 1982), (Lee, 1984), (Morgan, 1986); sterigmatocystin (Kang, 1984) and T-2 toxin (Pestka, 1981). In the application of ELISA in mycotoxin research several variants exist: the competitive assay, the titration assay (a sequential saturation variant of the competitive assay) and the inhibition assay (also indicated as immunometric assay). Their principles are concisely described hereafter:

Competition assay (see Figure 28)

A microtitre plate is coated with a known amount of antibody against the mycotoxin looked for (antigen). After being washed the test solution containing an unknown quantity of the mycotoxin, is added together with a known amount of enzyme-labelled mycotoxin. Labelled and non-labelled mycotoxin compete for the active sites of the found antibody. After incubation the plate is washed again and the captured enzyme is determined by adding chromogenic substrate. The intensity of the resulting colour can be measured photometrically, e.g. with an ELISA-reader, in which the microtitre plate can be placed. Measuring the colour or colour intensity can also be done visually. The lower the product concentration of the enzyme reaction, the lower the amount of bound enzyme and the higher the mycotoxin concentration in the test portion. Normally, determination of the amount of mycotoxin in the test solution is made by using a standard curve. An example of the competition assay is the Agriscreen[R] procedure of Neogen Corporation (1986), a commercial

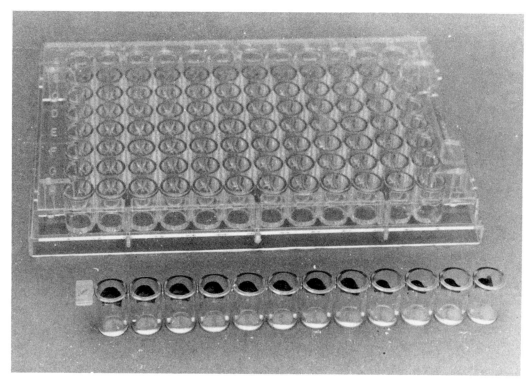

Figure 27. Microtitre plate and strip for Enzyme-linked Immunosorbent Assay.

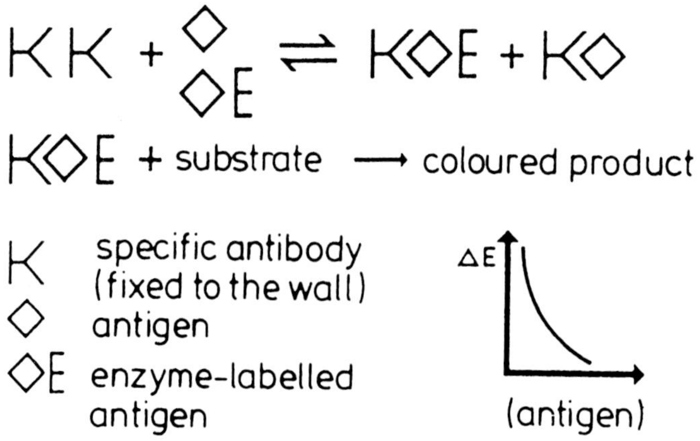

Figure 28. Principle of competition Enzyme-linked Immunosorbent Assay.

kit for screening foodstuffs and animal feedstuffs for aflatoxin B1 (see also section IV.D). In this kit factory-coated microtitre strips are supplied.

Titration assay (see Figure 29)

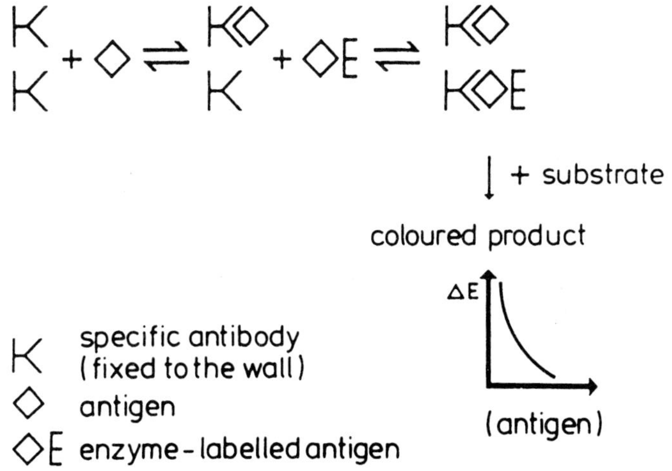

Figure 29. Principle of titration Enzyme-linked Immunosorbent Assay.

The titration assay is a sequential saturation variant of the competition assay. A microtitre plate is coated with a known amount of antibody against the mycotoxin looked for. After being washed, the test solution containing an unknown quantity of the mycotoxin is added. The mycotoxin to be measured reacts with a part of the coated antibodies. Then, the unbound antibodies are titrated with enzyme-labelled mycotoxin. The procedure then continues in the same way as the competititon assay. An example of the titration assay is the procedure of Biermann (1980 A,B) for the determination of aflatoxin B1 in foodstuffs.

Inhibition assay (see Figure 30)

In the inhibition assay the microtitre plate is coated with the mycotoxin and not with the antibody as is done in the competitive and titration assays. (The mycotoxin must be conjugated with a protein at first to make coating possible). The test solution containing an unknown quantity of mycotoxin and a fixed amount of antibody are added to the mycotoxin coated wells of the microtitre plate. The antibody that has not reacted with mycotoxin from the test-solution is captured by the mycotoxin-coated inside surface of the wells. This captured antibody is usually a rabbit immunoglobulin. After incubation and washing, the plate is incubated with a second (anti-rabbit) antibody, labelled with enzyme. In this way a kind of cascade is obtained: Enzyme-labelled antibody has reacted with anti-mycotoxin, antibody which, in turn, has bound to the mycotoxin coated on the well. The captured enzyme is determined by adding chromogenic substrate. The lower the product concentration of the enzyme reaction, the higher the mycotoxin concentration in the test portion. Again a standard curve is used for determination of the amount of mycotoxin in the test solution. The inhibition ELISA does not require an enzyme-labelled mycotoxin, however a mycotoxin-protein conjugate is needed to make coating possible to the wells of the microtitre plate. Enzyme-labelled anti-rabbit antibody is comercially available. An example of the inhibition assay is the procedure of Morgan (1982) for the determination of ochratoxin A (see Fig. 1) in barley.

In addition to the commercially available ELISA kits, an Enzyme Immuno Assay has become available for aflatoxins, in which "Quick-Cards[R]" are used instead of microtitre

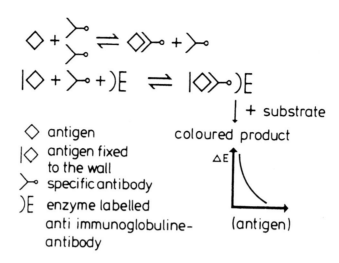

Figure 30. Principle of inhibition Enzyme-linked Immunosorbent Assay

plates or strips (International Diagnostics, 1987). In this "Quick-Card^R" procedure a controlled amount of anti-aflatoxin antibody is mounted onto each of two ports in a plastic card, that has the size of a credit card. A drop of aflatoxin-free control solution is added to the left port and a draft of the test solution is added to the right port. Enzyme-labelled aflatoxin is added to both card ports, followed by substrate solution. With increasing amounts of aflatoxin, the colour in the port will appear lighter in shade. Conversely, if no aflatoxin is present, a strong grey-blue dot will develop in the port. The aflatoxin-free control solution will render a dark grey-blue dot. The aflatoxin "Quick-Card^R" test is designed to detect levels of Aflatoxins B1, B2, G1 and M1 of approximately either 5 or 10 μg/kg. The procedure provides fast results and requires no equipment or technical experience to perform the test. The costs per analysis are low. The procedure has not yet (1987) been validated through a collaborative study. It is expected that commercial test card sets for the detection of zearalenone, deoxynivalenol and T2-toxin (see Fig. 1) will soon become available as well.

The extraction and clean-up procedures applied in Enzyme Immuno Assay for mycotoxins are generally simpler than those needed to apply chromatographic techniques. Often, methanol-water is used as an extraction solvent in aflatoxin Enzyme Immuno Assay, although methanol extractions are less efficient than chloroform in extracting aflatoxins (Trinder, 1985). Sometimes a simple defatting steps with hexane is applied, whereas column clean up is usually not necessary. Unlike many of the extracts prepared for chromatographic procedures, the final extracts used in Enzyme Immuno Assay are (buffered) aqueous solution.

ELISA-methods for mycotoxins validated by collaborative studies have not been published yet at the time of writing (1987). However the (provisional) results of the first AOAC-IUPAC collaborative study of an ELISA method (Agriscreen-procedure for the determination of aflatoxin B1 in some foodstuffs and animal feedstuffs) seem to be promising. (Park, 1987)

The simplicity of the ELISA's and the great many samples that can be handled in a day resulting in relatively low costs per analysis, have made the ELISA's of rapidly growing importance. The limits of detection of ELISA procedures for aflatoxins are sufficiently low to make determinations at the tolerance levels (van Egmond, 1987) for these components. On the other hand, ELISA procedures lead to more variation in test results than the conventional chromatographic procedures, and a matter of continuous vigilance is the specificity of ELISA's. Many mycotoxins have closely related chemical structures and are accordingly grouped together, e.g. the aflatoxins, ochratoxins and trichothecenes. Because of this there is, in principle, a possibility that cross-reactions could occur between antibodies evoked against a certain mycotoxin and other co-occurring toxins within the same group. In practice this seems to happen in some aflatoxin assays, where the antibody against aflatoxin B1 shows some crossreactivity with other aflatoxins. Consequently, a positive analysis result does not give selective information as to the concentrations of the separate aflatoxins. This is in contrast to TLC and HPLC, which allow distinguishing between the naturally occurring aflatoxins B1, B2, G1 and G2. It is to be expectd that ELISA's will become very valuable as rapid screening procedures in the determination of mycotoxins. However, at the moment ELISA-methods and -systems still have to undergo intensive validation processes, before their merits can be fully estimated.

b. Radio Immuno Assay

In the performance of Radio Immuno Assay (RIA), the formation of the antigen-antibody complex can be measured by using radiolabelled antigen in competitition with antigen to be determined. The mechanism of Radio Immuno Assay is outlined in Figure 31.

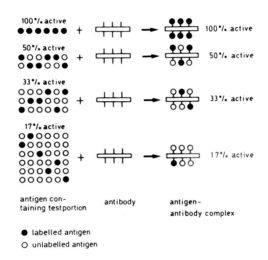

Figure 31. Mechanism of Radio Immuno Assay.

The test portion, containing a known amount of labelled antigen (marked as active) and an unknown amount of unlabelled antigen (the mycotoxin looked for), is brought into contact with a fixed amount of antibody. Competition takes place between labelled and unlabelled antigen for the active sites of the antibody. After a certain time equilibrium is reached, and there will remain some free antigen, the rest being bound to the antibody. The relative binding ratio of the labelled and unlabelled antigen to the antibody depends on the relative concentration ratio of the labelled and unlabelled antigen, the lower the radioactivity of the antigen-antibody complex. After separation of the antigen-antibody complex and the free fraction, the radio-activity of the complex is measured in a liquid scintillation counter. This radioactivity is a measure of the amount of unlabelled antigen (the mycotoxin looked for) in the test portion. Normally the evaluation of the amount of mycotoxin is an unknown sample is made by using a standard curve.

There exist only a few (published) RIA's in mycotoxin research: a method for the determination of aflatoxin B1 (Langone, 1976) and a method for the determination of T-2 toxin (Lee, 1981). This is probably due to the fact that the application of RIA requires laboratories to work with low concentrations of radioactive materials. Consequently, the application of RIA has some disadvantages such as limited shelflife activity of the radio isotopes, problems of radioactive waste disposal or licensing requirements and the need of an expensive scintillation counter. On the contrary, ELISA can be applied almost everywhere. This advantage, and the lower limits of detection achievable with ELISA (Chu, 1984) have stimulated the development of mycotoxin ELISA's rather than mycotoxin RIA's in the 1980's. Therefore, the RIA techniques will not be further discussed in this section.

Conclusion

The present state of methodology for the determination of mycotoxins in foodstuffs and animal feedstuffs may be summarized as follows:

1. Bioassays may be useful in tracing sources of known and unknown mycotoxins. However, their use in the surveillance of food and feedstuffs for mycotoxins is of minor importance.

2. Chemical assays are of major importance in the determination of mycotoxins. Most widely used are those techniques which include a chromatographic step to separate the mycotoxin of interest from matrix components.

3. Mini-column chromatographic procedures are useful as screening tests for agricultural commodities if quick decisions are needed as to whether to accept or reject a lot. They have been developed mainly for aflatoxins.

4. Thin layer chromatography (TLC), although a veteran in mycotoxin methodology, is a reliable, feasible and relatively simple separation technique with a broad field of application. It is a major technique to be used in the developing countries. Its two-dimensional application offers especially good resolution, resulting in low limits of detection.

5. High-performance liquid chromatography (HPLC) can be an attractive alternative to thin-layer chromatography. This more expensive technique offers the possibility of automating the ultimate separation and quantification steps. However, if the availability of service, spare parts and supplies form a problem as may be the case in many of the developing countries, TLC is to be preferred.

6. The use of gas chromatograph (GC) is limited mainly to the analysis of commodities for trichothecenes. Because these are of minor importance in developing countries and because GC may suffer from the same problems as HPLC, GCs of minor interest.

7. Enzyme-linked Immunosorbent Assay (ELISA) is a promising technique, which can be applied almost everywhere. Although still young, it is expected that ELISA will play an important role in screening for mycotoxins.

8. Radio Immuno Assays (RIA) will probably not become a major technique in mycotoxin determination, because of the disadvantages of working with radioactive materials.

Some characteristics of the various categories of methods discussed previously are compared to each other in Table 3. It should be realized that the classification of these categories is a rather subjective matter, influenced by personal experience, opinions and preferances and therefore debatable.

Table 3

Comparison of some characteristics of various categories of methods for the determination of mycotoxins in food

Category	Scope of Application	Reliability	Limits of detection	Equipment cost	Automation possible
Bioassay	Limited	Low	High	Low	No
Mini-column	Limited	Moderate	Moderate	Low	No
TLC	Broad	High	Low	Low	No
HPLC	Broad	High	Low	High	Partly
GC	Limited	High	Low	High	Partly
RIA	Limited	*	Low	High	Yes
ELISA	Limited	*	Low	Low	Yes

* Unknown at present.

7.   Performance characteristics

Methods of analysis have scientific and practical characteristics. The scientific characteristics determine the reliability of the analytical data, the practical characteristics determine the utility of the method. It depends on the purposes of the analyst which of these aspects deserves most attention. For research purposes and compliance activities it may be important that the true value be approached as closely as possible, and practical aspects may be of secondary consideration. Situations are also conceivable in which scientific elegance must be sacrificed for the benefit of practicality, for instance when rapid "go-no go" tests are required in the field to make a quick decision possible as whether to accept or reject a lot. Among the scientific characteristics of methods of analysis are the precision, accuracy, detectability, sensitivity and specificity, among the practical characteristics are the applicability, the cost of performance, the time and equipment required and the level of training needed. The properties of methods of analysis are also referred to as "method's performance characteristics" and "figures of merit". From the literature it is clear that there are many misunderstandings and incorrect usages of the scientific method's performance characteristics. It is therefore considered to be appropriate to define these terms.

Sensitivity

A quantitative analysis is only possible if there exists a relation of the measure x to the concentration c of the analyte (component being sought, for instance aflatoxin (s)). Such a relation is established by a series of calibration measurements, which yield the calibration function $x = f(c)$, its graph is called the analytical calibration curve (Fig. 32). In each point of this curve the sensitivity can be defined as $m = dx/dc$ which is the slope of the calibration curve (Kaiser, 1972), or in other words: the change in analytical signal per unit concentration change. It is the value that we need to know to make a quantification of the analyte on the basis of a certain analytical signal. Among analytical chemists it is frequently taken for granted in advance that the sensitivity for the analyte in the final sample extract is equal to the sensitivity for the analyte as present in a simple standard solution. This presumption may not always be true and should at least be checked. Matrix effects may give rise to an improper calibration of the determinative step of the method of analysis and consequently to estimates of the analyte which are either too high or too low.

The unit in which sensitivity is measured is the quotient of the units for the measure x and for the concentration c. Note that Sensitivity is not a concentration, nor does it indicate the smallest difference between concentrations that can be significantly distinguished by a method. The latter is a statistical matter, to which we shall come back in the paragraph "precision".

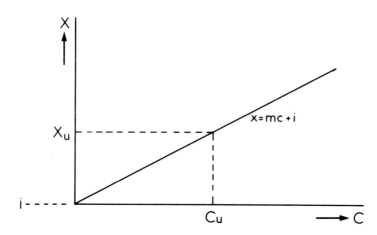

Figure 32. Analytical calibration curve of signal x versus concentration C.

Sensitivity should not be confused with "limit of detection" nor with related terms as detectability. The relation between sensitivity and limit of detection will be discussed in the paragraph "limit of detection".

Specificity

An analytical procedure is called "fully specific" when it gives an analytical signal solely for one particular component, but is "dead" for all other components, which may also be present in the sample (Kaiser, 1972). A fully specific procedure gives a zero chance of false-positives. Conventional analysis methods for mycotoxins using TLC and HPLC as techniques to separate the mycotoxins from other matrix components present in the final extract are often not fully specific, as other substances may be present which behave in the same way as these mycotoxins, even if two-dimensional TLC, a powerful separation technique, is used (see III-6). In order to minimize the risk of false-positives, the identity of the mycotoxin in positive samples has to be confirmed. The incorporation of several easy-to-carry-out confirmatory tests in the analysis procedures, for instance in **situ** derivative formation on thin layer plates or post-column derivatization in HPLC-systems have made the chromatographic analysis methods quite specific. Immunoassays for mycotoxin determination such as ELISA can be quite specific, especially since monoclonal antibodies are used.

Precision

Precision is a measure of variability. It relates to the unavoidable scatter between results obtained by applying a method of analysis in replication either within a laboratory or in different laboratories. A common description of precision is by the standard deviation or the relative standard deviation (= standard deviation/mean = coefficient of variation (C.V.)) of a set of replicate results. If the measurements are behaving normally, approximately two-thirds of them will be within 1 standard deviation on either side of the mean and about 95% of them will be within 2 standard deviations on either side of the mean. The precision may relate to the within laboratory error of a method, which can be expressed as the repeatability or to the between laboratory error of a method, which can be expressed as the reproducibility (ISO, 1981). The repeatability (r) can be defined as the value below which the absolute difference between two single test results obtained with the same method on identical test material, under the same conditions (same operator, apparatus, laboratory and short intervals of time) may be expected to lie with a specified probability. In the absence of other indication, the probability is 95%. Mathematically the repeatability r = 2.83 s , where s = standard deviation of the test results. The reproducibility (R) can be defined as the value below which the absolute difference between two single test results obtained with the same method on identical material, but under different conditions (different operators, apparatus, laboratories and/or different times) may be expected to lie with a specified probability. In the absence of other indication, the probability is 95%. Mathematically the reproducibility R = 2.83 s, where s = standard deviation of the test results. The repeatability and reproducibility of a method may be applied in various ways. They can serve:

- to verify that the experimental technique of a laboratory is up to standard
- to compare tests performed on a sample from a batch of material with a specification
- to compare test results obtained by various laboratories.

Information about the precision of a method (determination of repeatability and reproducibility) must be obtained through testing this method in an interlaboratory collaborative study (precision experiment), designed according to generally recognized guidelines (ISO, AOAC). In the case of aflatoxin assays, there have been many collaborative studies on methods that make use of TLC, so that a fairly good insight is obtained as to the precision aspects of these methods. As yet (1987) only few collaborative studies have been undertaken on aflatoxin methods that use HPLC in the determinative step, and only one of an ELISA-screening method for aflatoxin B1. Very interesting are the results of a retrospective study by Horwitz (1980, 1981) who investigated the precision data derived from ca. 200 collaborative studies, conducted under the auspices of the AOAC, among which were a number of aflatoxin studies. Two remarkable conclusions were drawn in general, that hold true for aflatoxin assays (TLC-assays) as well: 1) The interlaboratory precision (reproducibility) appears to be a function of concentration (Fig. 33) and seems to be independent of the nature of the analyte or the technique used for the measurement.

In general this precision can be represented by the following equation $C.V.(\%) = 2^{(1-0.5\log c)}$ where c is the concentration expressed as powers of 10 (e.g. 1 ppm = 10). 2) The ratio repeatability/reproducibility is mostly in between ca. 0.5 and 0.7. Ratio's <0.5 indicate a very personal method, analysts can check themselves well but they cannot check other analysts in other laboratories. This situation suggests that the directions require reworking or that the reference standards may differ from laboratory to laboratory. A ratio >0.7 can indicate that individual analyst replications are so poor that they eliminate the between-laboratory component.

These conclusions are of considerable practical importance. They mean that at a level of ca. 10 mg/kg, which is a "normal" contamination level for aflatoxin B1 a within laboratory C.V. of ca. 20% and a between laboratory C.V. of ca. 32% may be expected. In addition, at a level of 0.1 mg/kg, a "normal" contamination level for aflatoxin M1, a within laboratory C.V. of ca. 40% and a between laboratory C.V. of ca. 64% may be expected.

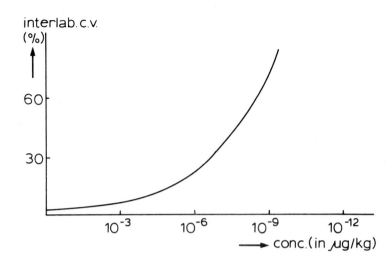

Figure 33. Interlaboratory coefficient of variation as a function of concentration.

Limit of detection

The limit of detection of a method is the lowest concentration level that can be determined to be statistically different from an analytical blank. Although this definition seems rather straightforward, significant problems have been encountered in expressing these values because of the various approaches to the term "statistically different".

IUPAC states that the limit of detection, expressed as a concentration cL is derived from the smallest measure xL , that can be detected with reasonable certainty for a given analytical procedure (see Fig. 34) (Kaiser, 1972, Long, 1983).

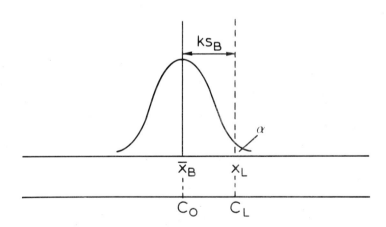

Figure 34. Normal distribution curve for a measured x variable.

Mathematically $xL = xB + 3.sB$ (1), where xB and sB are estimates of the mean value of the blank responses and the standard deviation of the blank responses respectively. Ultimately we are more interested in the lowest significant concentration cL than in the measure xL. If xL is known cL can be directly established through the calibration curve, in each point of which the sensitivity m is defined as $m = dx/dc$ (2) (see Sensitivity). By substituting equation (2) into equation (1) the relation between sensitivity and limit of detection becomes clear:

$$m = dx/dc \longrightarrow dc = dx/m$$

$$cL - cO = (xL - xB)/m$$

$$cL = 3sB/m$$

Near the limit of detection all quantitative determinations of a substance are rather imprecise. It is reasonable to set a minimum criterion for quantitative determinations at some distance away from the limit of detection. There are no definitions yet of this limit of determination or limit of quantitation, but the ACS Subcommittee on Environmental Analytical Chemistry has proposed to setting the limit of determination at $10.sB$ away from xB (ACS, 1980). Samples that are measured as having a signal x, where $x > 10.sB$ are termed to be in the region of quantitation then, while samples where $3.sB < x < 10.s$ are termed to be in the region of detection (Fig. 35).

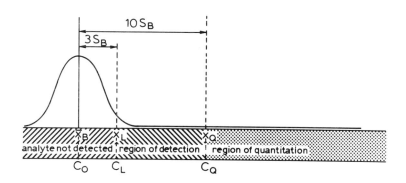

Figure 35. Regions of analyte measurement.

When TLC-techniques with simple visual estimation are applied, as will be often the case in most developing countries, it is not possible to establish the limit of detection according to this approach. In these cases, some authors relate their reported limit of detection to the lowest amount of mycotoxin visible on a TLC plate which means a level at which in 50% of the cases the mycotoxin will (not) be observed. Others establish their limit of detection with standards only or with "easy matrices" that cause no serious background in the detection step, whereas the limit of detection may depend strongly from the matrix being investigated. Further complications are the differences in intensities between the various types of UV-lamps and (in the case of instrumental techniques) differences in sensitivities between different HPLC-detectors. This all makes an objective comparison between reported limits of detection of various methods often difficult so that the provided data only give rough indications.

Accuracy

Accuracy (or bias) is a measure of systematic deviation from the true value. The smaller the systematic part of the experimental error the more accurate is the procedure. The accuracy of a method is usually expressed in terms of percentages of re covery. Theoretically the recovery of a method may never be > 100% as some of the analyte is always lost during an analysis, and thus the systematic error is directed in the negative way. In the practice of mycotoxin analysis, recoveries of 70-80% are common, however sometimes recoveries exceed 100%, probably as a result of persistant interferences.

For the determination of the accuracy a large number of analyses have to be made in order to smoothen the random part of the experimental error. Accuracy data of methods of analysis should be derived from collaborative studies through the calculation of the mean recovery of known amounts of added analyte which have been carried through the entire method (spiked samples). (Spiking should be done at levels in the order of magnitude of the expected levels or level-ranges of the analyte originally present in the sample). The weak point is that this test only applies when "pure" compounds are added. In the case of mycotoxins which are naturally occuring compounds, we have to presume that the recovered fraction of originally present mycotoxin in the sample is equal to that of added mycotoxin. Actually we do not know whether or not all the naturally mycotoxin is amenable to extraction by our initial solvents. The availability of certified reference materials in which mycotoxins are "naturally" present would partly overcome the problem (see Quality Assurance). At least the accuracy of the concerning method can be calculated then with the help of a "true value", agreed upon by certification. Again practice is more difficult because such certified reference materials for mycotoxin determinations are still in a development stage.

8. Quality Assurance

Many laboratories perform large numbers of determinations of aflatoxins and other mycotoxins and consider themselves to be experienced and reliable. We may reasonably ask ourselves then how it happens that laboratories so often find such different values even on samples which have been especially homogenised for collaborative studies. Further, those who have to meet the costs of these often expensive measurements may wonder which, if any, of the results they are to believe. Check Sample Programmes for mycotoxins, as organised by the International Agency for Research on Cancer have shown that large variability in results must be considered more as the norm than the exception (Friesen, 1982), a fact that gives little comfort to those who must either pay for the measurement or who base potentially important decisions upon them. However, this state of affairs must not be regarded as inevitable.

It has been proven that in general analysts contribute from one-half to two-third of the total variability of an analytical measurement system. Man is neither unbiased nor objective, therefore a laboratory working in the field of trace analysis should develop a Quality Assurance Programme. A Quality Assurance Programme should include various elements, among which:

a. Maintenance of skilled personnel, written and validated methods, and properly constructed, equipped and maintained laboratory facilities.

b. Use of high-quality glassware, solvents and other testing materials.

c. Frequent checking of the accuracy of chemical measurements.

The availability of the first two elements may depend on the location where the study will be carried out. Serious problems may be anticipated at some locations in developing countries where additional materials and scientific support may be needed, before a monitoring programme can be initiated. The third mentioned requirement may be hard to achieve and to demonstrate. However there exist several possible mechanisms for checking the accuracy. (Wagstaffe, 1987). These are summarized in Table 4.

For checking the reliability of test results by two or more independent methods, these methods must have been used successfully in similar analytical situations (same concentrations, similar interferences). By "independent" is meant measurements based upon different physico-chemical properties of the analyte, for instance TLC versus ELISA. The likelihood of two independent methods being biased by the same amount and in the same direction is very low. Therefore, when the analytical results agree, the results are with some certainty accurate. In-house independent method comparisons serve as a valuable function in a quality assurance programme.

Table 4

Some procedures for checking/improving the accuracy of chemical measurement
(after Wagstaffe, 1987)

Procedure	Comments
Cross check results within laboratory by fully independent method and analyst	Seldom possible for most laboratories; full independance hard to achieve
Participate in external Quality Assurance programme	Not always available when required: "true" value not always known to organizers
Use of certified reference material to check/improve accuracy of procedure	Convenient and economic; can be used when required; limited range of certified reference materials available

The International Agency for Research on Cancer (IARC) is conducting an on-going external Quality Assurance Programme (Friesen, 1982). Yearly samples of agricultural commodities to be analysed for aflatoxin B1, B2, G1 and G2 and milk products to be analysed for aflatoxins M1 are sent to a few dozens of countries, among which are several developing countries. Taking part in this IARC Mycotoxin Check Sample Survey Programme is free of charge and strongly recommended to every laboratory carrying out mycotoxin determinations.

The Community Bureau of Reference (BCR) of the European Communities currently undertakes a Mycotoxin Programme with the objective to improve the accuracy, and thereby, the comparability of mycotoxin measurements. This is realised by the development of certified reference materials (CRM's). In Table 5 the mycotoxins and matrices selected at the onset of the BCR Mycotoxin Programme are summarized (Wafstaffe, 1987). Recently, milk powders certified for their aflatoxin M1 content have become available.

These certified reference materials are available from the BCR in small units. Other mycotoxin reference materials, such as peanut meal with aflatoxin B1, are currently underway.

All of the components of the programmes to assure precision and accuracy add workload and expense to the laboratory. The time needed to put them into effect has been estimated to be ca. 30% of the total time available for analysis. Quality Assurance is, however, essential to guarantee the quality and integrity of analytical data.

Table 5

Summary of BCR mycotoxin matrix RM projects (after Wagstaffe, 1987)

Matrix:	Milk powder	Peanut meal + compound wheat feeds	
Mycotoxin:	Aflatoxin M1 certified .05;.31 and .76 mcg/kg	Aflatoxin B1, 10-40 mcg/kg	Deoxynivalenol 400 mcg/kg
Preparation:	Spray drying milk of cattle fed aflatoxin B1	"Naturally" encountered products	Natural and fungal-induced contamination

Note: Zearalenone and ochratoxin A will be undertaken in a third phase.

IV LABORATORY PROCEDURES

1. **Salt crystal liquefaction test for the determination of the water activity (aW) of agricultural products**

   (Procedure based upon the method of Northolt et al. J. Food Prot. 45, 537-540, 1982); Handbook on rapid detection of mycotoxins 3-7, OECD, Paris, 1982).

   ### Purpose and scope

   A method is described for measuring the water activity (aW) of foodstuffs. The test is suitable to check the aW of various agricultural products, which must comply with required aW standards in order to prevent fungal growth and the production of mycotoxins.

   ### Definition

   The water activity (aW) is defined as the equilibrium relative water vapour pressure of a substrate.

   $$aW = \frac{\text{water vapour pressure of substrate}}{\text{water vapour pressure of pure water}}$$
   (at same temperature)

   ### Principle

   Salt crystals attract water vapour and liquefy when they are placed in a jar containing a product with an aW above the specific aW of the salt, which equals the aW of the saturated salt solution. The aW of samples can be determined by using salts with appropriate specific aW.

   ### Reagents

   vaselin

   powdered salts, mesh 105-210 μm, choice of salts depending on a standards of samples to be tested.

CuCl2. 2H2O	(aW * =	0.684)
NaCl	(aW =	0.756)
NH4Cl	(aW =	0.790)
(NH4)2SO4	(aW =	0.807)
KCl	(aW =	0.856)
K2Cr2O4	(aW =	0.870)
BaCl2.2H2O	(aW =	0.910)
(NH4) H2PO4	(aW =	0.939)
K2SO4	(aW =	0.982)

* – aW values of saturated salt solutions measured at 18 degrees Celsius with a dewpoint meter which was calibrated using the generally accepted relationship between dewpoint and water vapour pressure (CRC Handbook of Chemistry and Physics).

   ### Apparatus

   Air-tight jar of ca. 500 ml with transparent lid

   Spatula, stainless steel.

Procedure

Place 40–80g of sample in the jar

Close the jar and equilibrate for at least two hours. The test using salts with an aW > 0.91 should be equilibrated in incubator with aW temperature which is equal or some degrees Celsius lower than the room temperature. The test using salts with an aW < 0.91 can be carried out in a room without large temperature variations.

Open the jar briefly and spread a very thin layer of vaselin on the inner surface of the lid.

Strew a few dozens of the appropriate crystals with the help of the spatula on the vaselin.

Close the jar and equilibrate for 3–24 hours (depending on the used salt, see table 6).

Observe the crystals to see whether they are liquefied or not. When 50% or more of the crystals are liquefied, the test result is regarded to be positive.

Expression of results

In case of a positive test 50% or more of the crystals of salt x are liquefied after 3–24 h depending on the type of salt, type of product and temperature (see Table 6). The aW of the sample can be expressed as:

aW (sample) > aW (salt x) + 0.02

Discussion

The salt crystal liquefaction test is very simple, nevertheless some precautions must be taken. The test using salts with a high specific aW (0.91) must be carried out in an incubator to prevent wrong results by sudden changes of temperature. The test using salts of 0.75–0.87 a can be carried out in a room without large temperature variations. When $CuCl_2.2H_2O$ crystals are applied, the test is not easily disturbed by sudden changes of temperature, and therefore it can be used as field method to check the a which may lead to mould growth. For instance peanuts, for which the Codex Alimentarius Committee on Food Hygiene has proposed an aW–standard of 0.70 to prevent contamination with aflatoxins.

Direct sunlight and heat radiation of the bottom or the lid of the jar must be prevented to avoid incorrect results. The sample should be 40–80 g because the aW of smaller samples may decrease due to loss of water vapour during filling and re–opening of the jar. False positive results may occur with larger samples when the temperature rapidly decreases, due to oversaturation of water vapour.

The sensitivity of the test is 0.04 aW with aW reading time of 2–7h, and 0.02 aW with a reading time of 3.24 h, depending on the type of salt, type of product and temperature.

It should be noted that the test gives an indication of the aW at the time of sampling only and not of the aW before. Therefore it cannot be excluded that the product has been contaminated with mycotoxins before.

Table 6

Liquefaction time of crystals of different salts
determined with different products at 18°C

Test material	aW (test material)	Salt	aW (test material)-aW (salt)	Liquefaction time[1] (h)
Peanuts shell	0.702	CuCl2.2H2O	0.018	4
Glycerol solution	0.776	NaCl	0.020	4
Pastry	0.814	NH4Cl	0.024	7
Pastry	0.838	(NH4)2SO4	0.031	3
Glycerol solution	0.876	KCl	0.020	7
Glycerol solution	0.890	K2CrO4	0.020	12
Pastry	0.928	BaCl2.2H2O	0.018	6
Fermented sausage	0.960	(NH4)H2PO4	0.021	4
Water	1.000	K2SO4	0.018	7-24[2]

[1]Time required for liquefaction of 50% of crystals.
[2]Liquefaction occurred between reading time 7 and 24 hours.

2. Thin Layer Chromatography Laboratory Techniques

Preparation of thin layer plates

a. Equipment and chemicals

Silica gel for thin layer chromatography
Glass stoppered conical flask of 300 ml
Aligning tray ca 112 x 22 cm
TLC-spreader with 0.25 mm or adjustable outlet slit
Five 20 x 20 cm glass plates, thickness 4 mm
Two 5 x 20 cm glass plates, thickness 4 mm
Storage rack for TLC plates
Oven at 110°C
Desiccator with active silica gel desiccant

b.   Procedure

Carefully clean glassplates with a detergent or concentrated soda-solution, rinse with distilled water and let dry. Plates should be free of grease.

Place plates flush to each other and to the long retaining edge of the aligning tray, place the small plates at the left and right-hand end of the line of plates as starting and finishing plates.

Weigh 30 g of silica gel into a conical flask, add the amount of water recommended by the manufacturer, shake vigorously for 1 minute, and pour into spreader with outlet slit in closed position.

Place spreader on the starting glass plate on the tray, rotate lever 180 degrees and immediately coat the five glass plates with 0.25 mm thickness of silica gel suspension in about 5-6 seconds. Let plates rest until gelled (ca 10 minutes).

Clean spreader immediately after completion of spreading by powerful water jet. Detach the screw cover at the end of the tube and remove the tube. Clean the unit thoroughly with a bottle brush, taking care that the rim of the outlet slit is not damaged with marks or scratches.

Insert coated plates in storage rack, store preferably overnight at room temperature and place rack in oven for one hour.

Check that thin layers are smooth and equally spread over the plates. Store in desiccator until just before use.

Preparation of standards

Primary mycotoxin standards are available from several commercial firms and scientific institutions. They may be obtained in various forms, e.g. as dry films, crystals, qualitative and quantitative standard solutions. In this section the description of the preparation of standards for thin layer chromatography is limited to AFLATOXINS. However, essentially the same principles and techniques are valid for the preparation of standards of other mycotoxins.

a.   Apparatus

Analytical microbalance, sensitivity of 0.001mg
Spectrophotometer, capable of measurements from 200-400 nm, with 1 cm quartz-face cells.
Calibrate spectrophotometer as follows:
Prepare three solutions of $K_2Cr_2O_7$ in H_2SO_4
(1) $K_2Cr_2O_7$, 0.25 mmol/L in H_2SO_4, 9 mmol/L (Dissolve 78 mg $K_2Cr_2O_7$ in 1.0L H_2SO_4, 9 mmol/L water).
(2) $K_2Cr_2O_7$, 0.125 mmol/L in H_2SO_4, 9mmol/L (Dilute 25 ml of (1) to 50 ml with H_2SO_4, 9 mmol/L water
(3) $K_2Cr_2O_7$, 0.0625 mmol/L in H_2SO_4, 9 mmol/L (Dilute 25 ml of (2) to 50 ml with H_2SO_4, 9 mmol/L water.

Determine the absorbance (A) of solutions (1), (2) and (3) at maximum absorption near 350 nm, against H_2SO_4, 9 mmol/L as solvent blank. Calculate the molar absorption coefficient (ε) at each concentration:

$$\varepsilon = \frac{A}{c.1} \quad \text{where c= concentration in mmol/L}$$

1 = pathlength in metres

If the three values vary by more than the guaranteed accuracy of the A scale, check either technique or instrument. Average the 3 ε values to obtain ε. Determine the correction factor (CF) for the instrument and cells by substituting in equation: CF = $\frac{316}{\varepsilon}$, where 316 = the value for ε of $K_2Cr_2O_7$ solutions (ε in m^2/mol).

If CF is < 0.95 or >1.05, check either instrument or technique to determine and eliminate the cause (use the same set of cells in calibration and determination of purity of mycotoxin standards).

b. Check of purity

Aflatoxins to be used as primary standards must meet following criteria of purity:

(1) chromatographic purity as determined below
(2) molar absorption coefficients within confidence limits given in table 7
(3) absorption peak ratios within confidence limits given in table 8

Weigh ca 1 mg aflatoxin standard using analytical microbalance and transfer quantitatively to a volumetric flask of 100 ml. Dissolve and dilute to volume with methanol. Calculate the concentration(c) of the solution in $\mu g/ml$. Measure the absorbance (A) of the solution at maximum absorption (see table 7). Calculate molar absorption coefficient(s):

$$\varepsilon = \frac{A \times MW}{c.l.}, \text{ where}$$

MW = molecular weight of the aflatoxin concerned (see table 9)
 c = concentration in mmol/L
 l = pathlength in m

Calculate ratios of absorbance for each aflatoxin at wavelengths given in table 8.

Table 7

Molar absorption coefficients (ε) of aflatoxins in methanol and 95% confidence limits expected from single determination of molar absorption coefficients

Aflatoxin	λ, nm	ε (m^2/mol) in MeOH	95% Confidence Limits ($\pm$)
B_1	223	2210	160
	265	1240	80
	360	2180	110
B_2	222	1860	100
	265	1210	60
	362	2400	50
G_1	216	2740	250
	242	960	30
	265	960	120
	362	1770	70
G_2	214	2530	230
	244	1050	30
	265	900	110
	362	1930	80

Table 8
Ratios of major peaks of UV absorption spectra of aflatoxins in
methanol and 95% confidence limits expected from single spectra

Major Peaks compared nm	Parameter	Aflatoxins			
		B_1	B_2	G_1	G_2
223/265	Ratio	1.77	1.54		
	95% Conf. limits	±0.04	±0.05		
214/265	Ratio			2.86	2.83
	95% Conf. limits			±0.15	±0.13
242/265	Ratio			1.00	1.20
	95% Conf. limits			±0.02	±0.07
362/265	Ratio	1.76	1.98	1.84	2.09
	95% Conf. limits	±0.04	±0.08	±0.06	±0.18

Table 9

Molecular Weight (MW) of some aflatoxins

Aflatoxin	MW
B_1	312
B_2	314
G_1	328
G_2	330
M_1	328

c.   **Preparation of TLC standards**

Preparation of stock solutions:

Aflatoxin standards received as dry films or crystals:
Add chloroform or benzene–acetonitrile (98 + 2) to the container of dry aflatoxin, calculated to give a concentration of 8–10 μg/ml. For aflatoxin M_1, use chloroform or benzene–acetonitrile (90 + 10). Use the label statement of aflatoxin weight as a guide. Vigorously agitate the solution for 1 minute on a Vortex shaker and transfer without rinsing to a convenient size glass stoppered flask.

Note: Do not dry aflatoxin for weighing or other purposes unless facilities are available to prevent dissemination of aflatoxins to surroundings due to electrostatic charge on particles.

Aflatoxin standards received as solutions:

Transfer the solution to a convenient glass stoppered flask. Dilute, if necessary, to a concentration of 8–10 μg/ml.

d.   **Determination of aflatoxin concentration:**

Record a UV spectrum of the aflatoxin solution obtained above from 330 to 370 nm against the solvent used for solution in the reference cell.   Determine the concentration of the aflatoxin solution by measuring the absorbance (A) at the wavelength of maximum absorption close to 350 nm and using the following equation:

$$\mu g \text{ aflatoxin/ml} = \frac{(A \times MW \times CF)}{1 \cdot \varepsilon}, \text{ where}$$

CF = correction factor obtained in calibrating the spectrophotometer
1 = pathlength in m.
MW is read from table 9 and ε-values (m^2/mmol) are as follows:

Aflatoxin	ε-(benzene-acetonitrile)	ε(chloroform)
B$_1$	1980	2100
B$_2$	2090	
G$_1$	1710	
G$_2$	1820	
M$_1$	1882	1995

Return the aflatoxin solution to the original glass stoppered flask (Normal exposure to UV light during absorbance measurement results in no observable conversion to photoproducts).

e.   **Determination of chromatographic purity:**

Onto a TLC plate, apply spot(s) of 5 μl of the standard solution(s) on an imaginary line, at a distance of ca 2 cm from the surface of the developing solvent. Develop the plate in one of the developing solvents indicated in table 10. Repeat the procedure with

Table 10

Developing solvents for TLC of aflatoxins

B$_1$,B$_2$, G$_1$ and G$_2$ = Order of Aflatoxin Rf from top:

chloroform-acetone (90 + 10), unsaturated tank
diethylether-methanol-water (96 + 3 + 1), unsaturated tank
diethylether-methanol-water (94 + 4.5 + 1.5), saturated tank
chloroform-methanol (94 + 6), saturated tank
chloroform-ethanol (97 + 3), saturated tank
benzene-methanol-acetic acid (90 + 5 + 5), unsaturated tank
dichloromethane-trichloroethene-n-amylalcohol-formic acid (80 + 15 + 4 +
    1), unsaturated tank (order of Rf changed to B$_1$, G$_1$, B$_2$, G$_2$).
chloroform-acetone-water ((88 + 12 + 1.5), unsaturated tank
chloroform-acetone-isopropanol-water (88 + 12 + 1.5 + 1), unsaturated
    tank
chloroform-isopropanol (99 + 1), unsaturated tank
toluene-ethylacetate-formic acid (6 + 3 + 1), unsaturated tank.

M$_1$:

diethylether-methanol-water (95 + 4 + 1), unsaturated tank
diethylether-hexane-methanol-water (85 + 10 + 4 + 1), unsaturated tank
chloroform-acetone methanol (90 + 10 + 2), unsaturated tank
chloroform-acetone-isopropanol (87 + 10 + 3), unsaturated tank

a second plate, developed in a different solvent system, indicated in table 10. In UV-light, the chromatograms shall show only the spot(s) of the individual aflatoxin standard(s), and no other fluorescence shall be perceptible.

f.   Preparation and storage of standard solution(s):

Dilute a portion of the stock solution away from daylight, with the same solvent as used for the stock solution, to obtain a standard solution with a concentration as prescribed in the analysis procedure concerned (usually 0.1 or 0.5 μg aflatoxin/ml). After aliquots have been removed for dilution or spotting, weigh the flask containing the stock solution to the nearest mg and record the weight for future reference, before storage of the stock solution.

Wrap the flask tightly in aluminium foil and store at <4°C, but not at 0°C for chloroform solutions. When the solution is to be used after storage, reweigh the flask and record any change. To avoid incorporation of water condensation, bring the stock solution as well as the standard solution to room temperature before use. Do not remove Al-foil from the flask until the content has reached room temperature. The stock solution can be saved for 4 months, if stored excluded from light in a refrigerator. The standard solution can be saved at least 14 days if stored in the same way.

g.   Preparation of resolution reference standard:

Prepare resolution reference standard by mixing aflatoxins B_1, B_2, G_1 and G_2 solutions, to give concentrations at final dilution with[1] chloroform of benzene-acetonitrile at ca 1, 0.4, 1 and 0.4 μg/ml respectively.

Thin layer chromatography

a.   Spotting and development

In TLC analysis of mycotoxins, the substances that are applied to the plate generally have volumes ranging from ca 5-25 μl. Depending on the desired accuracy and precision one may use different types of applicators, such as qualitative capillary pipettes, quantitative capillary pipettes or precision syringes.

On the same TLC plate aliquot(s) of sample as well as aliquot(s) of the standard solution are applied directly after each other, keeping spots small and uniformly sized. In this way comparison of sample and standard is possible and justified, as both undergo the same developing conditions and possible plate to plate variations are eliminated. It is a good laboratory practice to apply samples and standards as rapidly as possible in subdued incandescent light, preferably under inert atmosphere to prevent decomposition. For visual estimation it is necessary that the intensity of sample spot(s) falls within the range of intensities of an increasing series of standard spots. Therefore, if samples of unknown concentrations of mycotoxin are analysed, it is useful to carry out preliminary TLC at first to establish the approximate mycotoxin content, so that a suitable dilution can be made for quantitative TLC. For densitometric quantitation dilutions have to be made if sample and standard spots have intensities of different orders of magnitude.

Development of the plates should be carried out in the dark or in subdued light as exposure of mycotoxins on adsorbent surfaces to (UV) light may lead to decomposition, particularly in presence of solvents. Likewise, TLC plates should be covered with a clean glass plate after evaporation of the solvent and stored in the dark, until visualization or determination. Exposure of developed spots to UV light should be for minimal time needed for visualization only. In order to obtain developing conditions as equal as possible, it is advisable to place two plates at the same time in the same tank, facing the coated sides to each other.

b.   Interpretation and calculation

The way mycotoxins are detected depends on the physico-chemical properties of the mycotoxin involved. Aflatoxins strongly absorb UV light and emit the energy of the absorbed UV light as fluorescent light. This fortunate characteristic enables the analyst to detect these components. For other mycotoxins visualization reagents must be used, for instance by spraying a reagent on the plate or by exposing the plate to reagent vapour.

After visualization the chromatogram must be interpreted to establish whether or not the mycotoxin of interest is present in the sample. The mycotoxin spot from the extract(s) can be located with the help of the co-developed standards. The presumed toxin spot should coincide with the reference standard in Rf-value and hue (colour). In case the interpretation of the chromatogram is hampered by the presence of other spots with similar Rf values as the presumed toxin spot, or when one has doubts about the identity of a "presumed" toxin spot, supplementary chromatography is advised. In such supplementary chromatography the TLC procedure is repeated, now with an internal standard, superimposed on the extract spot before developing the plate. After completion of TLC this superimposed standard and the "presumed" toxin spot from the sample must coincide.

Note: In two dimensional TLC the actual location of the mycotoxin spot from the sample extract after development in the second direction may be at a somewhat higher Rf value that that of the corresponding standard in the side lane. This is usually due to residues of the components of the first developing solvent (methanol, water) in the silica gel. These residue are not present in the side lane due to the solvent limit line. A slight discrepancy in Rf values may thus result.

Determination may be done visually or densitometrically, depending on the facilities available at the laboratory. In visual estimation, the intensity of the toxin spot(s) of the sample(s) is (are) compared with those of the standards and it is determined which of the standard spots matches the sample spot. If necessary an interpolation is made. The calculation of the concentration of the mycotoxin in the sample is made using the following fomula:

$$\mu g/kg = \frac{S \times Y \times V}{X \times W}$$

where: S = μl of mycotoxin standard equal to unknown
       Y = concentration of mycotoxin standard in μg/ml
       V = μl of final dilution of sample extract
       X = μl sample extract giving a spot intensity equal to S
       W = mass of the sample, represented by the final extract in g.

In densitometric determination, the intensities of sample and standard spot(s) are scanned according to the instructions of the manufacturer, and the peak areas from the recorder printout are compared. In the case of two dimensional TLC it is usual to scan the standard spots developed in the second direction. The calculation of the concentration of the mycotoxin in the sample is made using the following formula:

$$\mu g/kg = \frac{B \times Y \times S \times V}{Z \times X \times W}$$

where: B = average area of mycotoxin peak from sample
       Y = concentration of mycotoxin in standard in μg/ml
       S = μl of mycotoxin standard equal to unknown
       V = μl of final dilution of sample extract
       Z = average area of mycotoxin peak from standard
       X = μl sample extract spotted
       W = mass of samplem, represented by the final extract in g.

Confirmation of Identity

a. General principles

In spite of all cleanup techniques used, there are still substances which behave like the mycotoxin looked for in TLC separation. In order to minimize the possibility of false-positives, the identity of the mycotoxin in positive samples has to be confirmed. The most reliable method for this purpose is high resolution mass spectroscopy (MS). MS in combination with TLC however is rather time consuming and not every laboratory is equipped with this sophisticated type of apparatus. Therefore simple chemical techniques are preferred. These techniques do not offer the same absolute certainty as MS, but they exclude most false-positives.

Confirmatory tests for mycotoxins are generally based on derivatization of the mycotoxin of interest into a reaction product with specific chromatographic behaviour and/or colour. Both mycotoxin standard and suspected sample are submitted to the same derivatization reaction. Consequently, in positive samples a derivative from the mycotoxin should appear, identical to the derivative from the mycotoxin standard. Confirmatory reactions may be carried out in test tubes or, preferably, directly on a TLC plate, thus using the advantages of TLC. Examples of the latter possibility are the procedures for the confirmation of aflatoxin B1, originally developed by Przybylski (1975) and Verhülsdonk (1977), now adopted as official method by AOAC and EC respectively. In both methods aflatoxin B_1 is derivatized under acid conditions on a TLC plate into its hemiacetal aflatoxin B_2a, which has a blue fluorescence at a lower Rf than B_1.

In the (simple) method of Przybylski this is achieved by superimposing trifluoroacetic acid directly on the extract spot before development. After reaction the plate is developed and examined under UV-light for presence of the blue fluorescent spot of B_2a, which can be recognized with the help of a B_1 standard, spotted on the same plate, which underwent the same procedure. As an additional confirmation, H_2SO_4 is sprayed on another part of the plate where unreacted aliquots of extract and B_1 standard were developed. The H_2SO_4 acid spray changes the fluorescence of aflatoxin from blue to yellow. This test only confirms the absence of aflatoxins; i.e. spots which do not turn yellow are positively not aflatoxin, whereas many materials other than aflatoxin may give a yellow spot with H_2SO_4.

In the case of very "dirty" extracts it may be difficult to notice the hemi-acetal of B_1 (B_2a) due to heavy background fluorescence. Then the twoonal method of Verhülsdonk should be the method of choice, in which a so called separation-reaction-separation technique is carried out. Hydrochloric acid is sprayed after the first separation run, the reaction takes place. Then a second separation is carried out in the second dimension, under exactly identical conditions, after which the isolated blue fluorescent spot of B_2a is visible, which can be recognized with the help of a B_1 standard, spotted on the same plate and which underwent the same procedure. Other (unreacted) components lie on a diagonal line, bisecting the plate, as the separation was carried out in both directions under exactly identical conditions.

Note: Both methods work equally well for confirmation of the identity of aflatoxin G_1.

b. AOAC-method for aflatoxin B_1 (one dimensional)

Equipment and chemicals:

TLC-plates prepare as previously described or use ready made plates with 0.25 mm thick layer of silica gel (Merck, DC-Kiesel gel 60 (Darmstadt, GFR); Machery & Nagel, MN-G-HR (Düren, GFR); or equivalent).

Trifluoroacetic acid (TFA). Store in tightly closed bottle in refrigerator.
Microsyringe of 10 μl or quantitative glass capillaries.
Qualitative glass capillaries 1 μl.

Clean glass plate with dimensions of ca 10 x 20 cm.
Hot air blower.
Developing solvent: mixture of chloroform and acetone (85 + 15).
Rectangular developing chamber with glass edging and ground-glass cover or equivalent.
Longwave (360 nm) UV-lamp (use with UV-absorbing eye glasses) or ChromatoVue cabinet (Ultra-Violet Products, Inc.) or equivalent. The intensity of irradiation must make it possible for a spot of 1 ng of aflatoxin B_1 to be still clearly distinguished on a TLC plate at a distance of 10 cm from the lamp.

Procedure:
(See figure 36). Divide a TLC plate in two equal sections by scoring a thick line down the plate. Cover one section with the glass plate.
On the uncovered side, spot two aliquots of sample extract prepared for TLC containing 0.5 – 5ng aflatoxin B_1. Spot two aliquots of aflatoxin B_1 standard (of approximately the same amount as present in the sample) on one of these sample spots and on a separate place respectively.

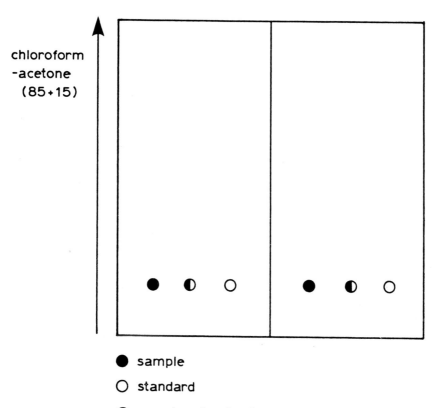

● sample
○ standard
◐ sample + standard

Figure 36

Superimpose 1 μl TFA on each of the three spots and let react for 5 minutes. Then blow warm air over the plate $\geq$ 10 minutes (the temperature of the air at the place surface should be ca 40°C). Uncover the second section of the plate and repeat the procedure described above. Do not add TFA.

Place a sufficient amount of the developing solvent in the developing tank and insert the plate in the tank. Place a trough or three small beakers containing water in front of the plate. Do not equilibrate. After development, examine the plate under longwave UV light. Unreacted aflatoxin B_1 appears near the top of the plate on the section without TFA. Blue fluorescent derivates (B_2a) from the B_1-standard and the extract with superimposed B_1-standard appear at a Rf of ca 0.25 on the section sprayed with TFA. Presence of aflatoxin B_2a in the channel of the reacted sample extract is proof of identity of aflatoxin B_1 in the sample extract.

3. **Thin layer chromatographic methods for the determination of Aflatoxin B1 in food-stuffs and animal feeding stuffs**

(Note: These procedures are based upon the official method of the European Communities, Off. J. Europ. Comm. L102, 9-18 (1976), text modified by P.L. Schuller and H.P. van Egmond).

One dimensional TLC procedure

a. **Purpose and scope**
The method makes it possible to determine the level of aflatoxin B_1 in the following simple feeding stuffs: cakes and meals prepared from groundnut, copra, linseed, soya, sesame, babassu palm, manioc and maize germ oil as well as cereals and cereal products, maize, pea meal, potato pulp, and starch. Although not specified in the scope of the official text of the EC-procedure, the method is also suitable for the analysis of various foodstuffs for aflatoxin B_1.

The lower limit of determination is ca 0.01 mg/kg (10 ppb).

If the presence of interfering substances hinders the determination, it is necessary to start the analysis again using two dimensional thin layer chromatography.

b. **Principle**

The test portion is subjected to extraction with chloroform. The extract is filtered, and an aliquot portion is taken and purified by column chromatography on silica gel. The eluate is evaporated and the residue redissolved in a specific volume of chloroform or of a mixture of benzene and acetonitrile. An aliquot portion of this solution is subjected to thin layer chromatography (TLC). The quantity of aflatoxin B_1 is determined under UV irradiation of the chromatogram, either visually or by fluorodensitometry, by comparison with known quantities of standard aflatoxin B_1. The identity of the aflatoxin B_1 extracted from the feeding stuff is confirmed by formation of the hemiacetal of aflatoxin B_1 on the TLC plate.

c. **Reagents**

(NB: All reagents shall be of "analytical reagent" quality).

Acetone.

Chloroform, stabilized with 0.5 to 1.0% of ethanol 96% (v/v).

n-Hexane.

Methanol.

Anhydrous diethyl ether, free from peroxides.

Mixture of benzene and acetonitrile: 98/2 (v/v).

Mixture of chloroform and methanol: 97/3 (v/v).

Silica gel, for column chromatography, particle size 0.05 to 0.20 mm.

Absorbent cotton wool, previously defatted with chloroform, or glass wool.

Sodium sulphate, anhydrous, granular.

Inert gas, e.g. nitrogen.

Hydrochloric acid, (1 mol/L).

Sulphuric acid, 50% (v/v) solution in water.

Diatomaceous earth (Kieselguhr, Hyflosupercel), acid-washed.

Silica gel G-HR or equivalent, for self coated plates.

Standard solution containing 0.1 μg of aflatoxin B_1 per ml in chloroform or the mixture of benzene and acetonitrile prepared and checked as described below.

Preparation of standard solution and determination of concentration:

Prepare a standard solution of aflatoxin B_1 in chloroform or the mixture of benzene and acetonitrile with a concentration of 8 to 10 μg/ml. Record the absorption spectrum between 330 and 370 nm with the aid of the spectrophotometer.

Measure the absorbance (A) at 353 nm in the case of the chloroform solution; and at 348 nm in the case when the solution is a mixture of benzene and acetonitrile.

Calculate the mass concentration in micrograms of aflatoxin B_1 per ml of solution from the formulae below:

$$\frac{312.A.1000}{20600} \qquad \text{for the chloroform solution;}$$

$$\frac{312.A.1000}{19800} \qquad \text{for the solution in the mixture of benzene and acetonitrile.}$$

Dilute the standard solution as appropriate, away from day light, to obtain a working standard solution with a concentration of aflatoxin B_1 of 0.1 μg/ml. If kept in a refrigerator at 4°C, this solution is stable for two weeks.

Testing of chromatographic purity of the standard solution:

Spot on a plate 5 μl of the standard solution of aflatoxin B_1 containing 8 to 10 μg/ml. Develop the chromatogram as indicated in 5.4.[1] In UV light the chromatogram shall show only one spot and no fluorescence shall be perceptible in the original deposit zone.

Standard solution for qualitative testing purposes containing about 0.1 μg of aflatoxin B_1 and B_2 per ml in chloroform or the mixture of benzene and acetonitrile. These concentrations are given as a guide. They shall be adjusted so as to obtain the same intensity of fluorescence for both aflatoxins.

Developing solvents:

Mixture of chloroform and acetone: 9/1 (v/v), unsaturated tank;

Mixture of diethyl ether and methanol and water: 96/3/1 (v/v/v), unsaturated tank;

Mixture of diethyl ether and methanol and water: 94/4.5/1.5 (v/v/v), saturated tank;

Mixture of chloroform and methanol: 94/6 (v/v), saturated tank.

Mixture of chloroform and methanol: 97/3 (v/v), saturated tank.
Trifluoroacetic acid (store in tightly closed bottle in refrigerator).

Propanol-2.

Developing solvents for confirmatory test:

Mixture of chloroform and acetone and methanol (3.4): 90/10/2 (v/v/v), unsaturated tank;

Mixture of chloroform and acetone and propanol-2: 85/12.5/2.5 (v/v/v), unsaturated tank.

Sodium hypochlorite (NaOCl), 5% (v/v) solution in water.

d. Apparatus

Grinder-mixer.

Shaking apparatus or magnetic stirrer.

Fluted filter papers, Schleicher and Schüll No. 588 or equivalent, diameter: 24 cm.

Glass tube for chromatography (internal diameter: 22 mm; length: 300 mm), with a Teflon cock and a reservoir of 250 ml.

Rotary vacuum evaporator, with a round-bottomed flask of 500 ml.

Conical flask of 500 ml, with ground-glass stopper.

TLC apparatus.

Glass plates for TLC, 200 x 200 mm, prepared as follows (the quantities indicated are sufficient to cover five plates): Put 30 g of silica gel G-HR into a conical flask. Add 60 ml of water, stopper and shake for a minute. Spread the suspension on the plates so as to obtain a uniform layer 0.25 mm thick. Leave to dry in the air and then store in a desiccator containing silica gel. At the time of use, activate the plates by keeping them in an oven at $110^{\circ}C$ for one hour.

Precoated plates are suitable if they give results similar to those obtained with the plates prepared as indicated above.

Long-wavelength (360 nm) UV lamp. The intensity of irradiation shall make it possible for a spot of 1.0 ng of aflatoxin B_1 to be clearly distinguished on a TLC plate at a distance of 10 cm from the lamp.

WARNING — UV LIGHT IS DANGEROUS TO THE EYES. PROTECTIVE GOGGLES MUST BE WORN.

10 ml graduated tubes with glass or polyethylene stoppers.

UV spectrophotometer.

Fluorodensitometer (optional).

Capillaries of 1 or 2 microlitres or preferably a microsyringe (0–50 μl).

Spray unit for TLC (low volume capacity (5–20 ml)).

e.   **Procedure**

Preparation of the test sample:

Grind the laboratory sample so that it completely passes through a sieve with a 1 mm mesh (in accordance with recommendation ISO R 565).

Extraction:

Put 50 g of ground, homogenized test sample into a conical flask.   Add 25 g of diatomaceous earth, 25 ml of water and 250 ml of chloroform.   Stopper the flask, shake or stir for 30 minutes using the apparatus and filter through a fluted filter paper.   Discard the first 10 ml of the filtrate and then collect at least 50 ml.

Column clean-up:

Insert into the lower end of the chromatography tube a cotton or glass wool plug, fill two-thirds of the tube with chloroform and add 5 g of sodium sulphate.

Check that the upper surface of the sodium sulphate layer is flat, then add 10 g of silica gel in small portions.   Stir carefully after each addition to eliminate air bubbles.   Leave to stand for 15 minutes and then carefully add 15 g of sodium sulphate.   Open the tap, allow the liquid to flow until it is just above the upper surface of the sodium sulphate layer.   Close the tap.

Mix 50 ml of the extract collected in 5.2 with 100 ml of n-hexane and quantitavely transfer the mixture to the column.   Open the tap, allow the liquid to flow until it is just above the upper surface of the sodium sulphate layer.   Close the tap. Discard this washing.   Then add 100 ml of diethyl ether and again allow the liquid to flow until it is just above the upper surface of the sodium sulphate layer. During these operations see that the rate of flow is 8 to 12 ml per minute and ensure that the column does not run dry. Discard the liquid that comes out.   Then elute with 150 ml of the mixture of chloroform and methanol and collect the whole of the eluate in the round-bottomed flask of the rotary evaporator.

Evaporate the eluate almost to dryness at a temperature not exceeding 50°C and preferably under a stream of inert gas under reduced pressure with the rotary evaporator.   Quantitatively transfer the residue, using chloroform or the mixture of benzene and acetonitrile, to a 10 ml graduated tube.   Concentrate the solution under a stream of inert gas and then adjust the volume to 2.0 ml with chloroform or the mixture of benzene and acetonitrile.

NOTE –   Aflatoxin B_1 is a highly carcinogenic substance and shall therefore be handled very carefully. Do not transfer dry aflatoxin for weighing or other purposes unless facilities (e.g. glove box) are available to prevent dissemination of aflatoxin to surroundings due to electrostatic charge on particles.   Rinse all glassware exposed to aflatoxin carefully with chloroform, then with the solution of NaOCl bleach and then wash thoroughly. Swab accidental spills of aflatoxin with the solution of NaOCl bleach.   For more details on decontamination procedures see IARC Publication No. 37 "Laboratory decontamination and destruction of aflatoxins B_1, B_2, G_1, G_2 in laboratory wastes" editors M. Castegnaro et al, Lyon 1980.

Thin layer chromatography:

Spot on a TLC plate, 2 cm from the lower edge and at intervals of 2 cm, the volumes indicated below of the standard solution and the extract of the test portion using capillary pipettes or the microsyringe.

- 10, 15, 20, 30 and 40 μl of the standard aflatoxin B_1 solution;

- 10 μl of the extract obtained in 5.3. and, superimposed on the same point, 20 μl of the standard solution;

- 10 and 20 μl of the extract obtained above.

Dry in a slow stream of air or inert gas. The spots obtained shall have a diameter of about 5 mm.
Develop the chromatogram in the dark with one of the developing solvents. (The choice of the solvent shall be made before-hand, by depositing 25 μl of the qualitative standard solution on the plate and checking that, when developed, the blue fluorescent aflatoxins B_1 and B_2 are completely separated). Allow the solvent to evaporate in the dark and then irradiate with UV light, placing the plate 10 cm from the lamp. The spots of aflatoxin B_1 show a blue fluorescence.

Determination:

Estimate visually or determine by fluorodensitometry as indicated below.

Visual estimation:

Estimate the quantity of aflatoxin B_1 in the extract by comparing the intensities of fluorescence of the extract spots with that of the standard solution spots. Interpolate if necessary. The fluorescence obtained by the superimposition of the extract on the standard solution shall be more intense than that of the 10 μl of extract and shall be perceptible as only one visible spot. If the intensity of fluorescence given by the 10 μl of extract is greater than that of the 40 μl of standard solution, dilute the extract 10 or 100 times with chloroform or the mixture of benzene and acetonitrile before repeating TLC.

Measurement by fluorodensitometry:

Measure the intensity of fluorescence of the aflatoxin B_1 spots with the fluorodensitometer at an excitation wavelength of 365 nm and an emission wavelength of 443 nm. Determine the quantity of aflatoxin B_1 in the extract spots by comparing the intensities of fluorescence of the extract spots with that of the standard aflatoxin B_1 spots. If the intensity of fluorescence given by the 20 μl of extract is considerably greater than that of the 40 μl of standard solution, dilute the extract 10 or 100 times with chloroform or the mixture of benzene and acetonitrile before repeating TLC.

Confirmation of the identity of aflatoxin B_1:

Confirm the identity of the aflatoxin B_1 in the extract by the presumptive test with sulphuric acid and, if the result of this test is positive, by the actual confirmation tests below using two-dimensional TLC. If the result of the presumptive test with sulphuric acid is negative, there is no need to proceed with the actual confirmation since, in this case, no aflatoxin B_1 is present.

Presumptive test with sulphuric acid:

Spray sulphuric acid on the chromatogram. The fluorescence of the aflatoxin B_1 spots shall turn from blue to yellow under UV irradiation.

Two-dimensional chromatography involving the formation of aflatoxin B_1-hemiacetal (aflatoxin B_{2a}) using hydrochloric acid: (This method is preferred in the case precoated plates and a spray cabinet with suction are available).

Application of the solutions (follow the diagram in Figure 37):

Inscribe two straight lines on a plate parallel to two contiguous sides (6 cm from each side) to limit migration of the solvent fronts. Spot the following solutions on the plate using capillary pipettes or the microsyringe.

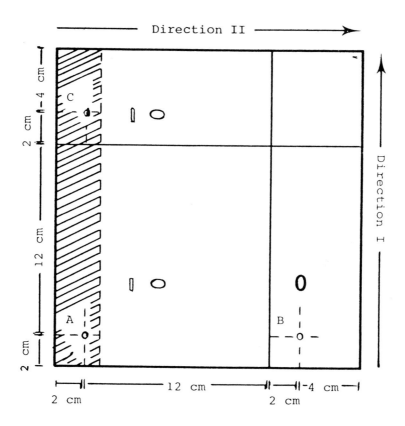

A : extract of test portion

B and C: aflatoxin B_1 standard

Figure 37

- at point A: a volume of extract of the test portion, obtained in 5.3., containing about 2.5 ng of aflatoxin B_1;

- at points B and C: 25 μl of the standard solution.

Dry in a slow stream of air or inert gas. The spots shall have a diameter of about 5 mm.

Development (follow the diagram in Figure 37):

Develop the plate in direction I, in the dark, using the developing solvent until the solvent front reaches the solvent limit line.

Remove the plate from the tank and allow to dry in the dark at ambient temperature for five minutes. Then spray hydrochloric acid along a band 2.5 cm broad, with the help of the spray unit, covering points A and C (indicated by the hatched area in figure 37) until it darkens, protecting the rest of the plate with a glass sheet. Allow to react for 10 minutes in the dark and dry with a stream of air at ambient temperature.

Next, develop the plate in direction II, in the dark, using the developing solvent until the solvent front reaches the solvent limit line. Remove the plate from the tank and allow to dry at ambient temperature.

Interpretation of the chromatogram:

Examine the chromatogram under UV light and check for the following features.

(1) Appearance of a blue fluorescent spot of aflatoxin B_1 originating from the standard solution applied at B (migration in direction I).

(2) Appearance of a blue fluorescent spot of unreacted (with the hydrochloric acid) aflatoxin B_1 and a more intense blue fluorescent spot of aflatoxin B_1-hemiacetal at a lower R_f-value, both originating from the standard solution applied at C (migration in direction II).

(3) Appearance of spots matching those described in (b), originating from the extract of the test portion applied at A. The position of these spots is defined first by the migration distance of the aflatoxin B_1 from point A in direction I (the same as that travelled by the standard applied at B), and then by the migration distances from there in direction II of the aflatoxin B_1-hemiacetal (the same as those travelled by the standard applied at C). The intensities of fluorescence of the hemiacetal spots originating from the extract and from the standard applied at C shall match.

Two-dimensional chromatography involving the formation of aflatoxin B_1-hemiacetal (aflatoxin B_{2a}) using tri-fluoroacetic acid:

Application of the solutions (follow the diagram in Figure 38):

Inscribe two straight lines on a plate parallel to two contiguous sides (6 cm from each side), to limit migration of the solvent fronts. Spot the following solutions on the plate using capillary pipettes or the microsyringe.

- at point A, a volume of the extract of the test portion obtained in 5.3., containing about 2.5 ng of aflatoxin B_1;

- at points B and C, 20 μl of the standard solution.

Dry in slow stream of air or inert gas. The spots obtained shall have a diameter of about 5 mm.

<u>Development</u> (follow the diagram in Figure 38):

A   : extract of test portion

B and C: aflatoxin B$_1$ standard

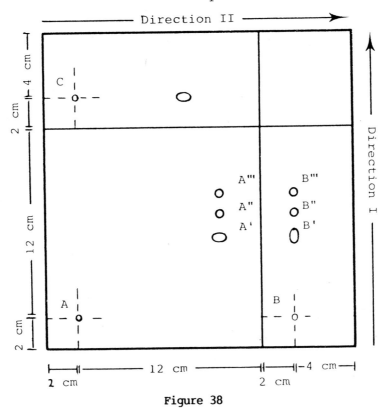

Figure 38

Develop the plate in direction I, in the dark, using the developing solvent until the solvent front reaches the solvent limit line. Remove the plate from the tank and allow to dry in the dark at ambient temperature for 15 minutes.

Then develop the plate in direction II, in the dark, using the developing solvent until the solvent front reaches the solvent limit line. Remove the plate from the tank and allow to dry, in the dark, at ambient temperature.

Examine the chromatogram under UV light and mark the locations of the spot from the standard solution at point B' (see Figure 38) and of the assumed aflatoxin B$_1$ spot (A') from the extract with a soft pencil. Spot with a glass capillary 1-2 μl trifluoracetic acid on the spots A' and B'. Dry with a stream of air at ambient temperature.

Develop the plate again in direction I (see Figure 38), in the dark, using one of the developing solvent mentioned earlier, until the solvent front reaches the solvent limit line again. Remove the plate from the tank and allow to dry, in the dark, at ambient temperature for 15 minutes.

<u>Interpretation of the chromatogram</u> (follow the diagram in Figure 38):

Examine the chromatogram under UV light and check for the following features:

(a) Appearance of a weak blue fluorescent spot of unidentified aflatoxin B_1-derivative (position B''') and a more intense blue fluorescent spot of aflatoxin B_1-hemiacetal (position B''), both originating from the standard aflatoxin B_1 (position B').

(b) Appearance of blue fluorescent spots (positions A''' and A''), originating from the assumed aflatoxin B_1 in the extract (position A'), which R_f-values correspond with both originating from the standard aflatoxin B_1 (position B').

The identity of aflatoxin B_1 in the extract is confirmed when the R_f-values of the aflatoxin B_1-hemiacetal spots from extract and standard (position A'' and B'' respectively) correspond.

f. Calculation of the results

Visual estimation:

The content in micrograms of aflatoxin B_1 per kg of sample (ppb) is given by the formula:

$$\frac{X.S.V}{Y.m}$$

in which:

X and Y are respectively the volumes in microlitres of the standard solution of aflatoxin B_1 and of the extract having a similar intensity of fluorescence;

S = mass concentration in micrograms of aflatoxin B_1 per ml of the standard solution;

V = final volume of the extract in microlitres, taking into account any dilution that was necessary;

m = mass in grammes of the test portion correspnding to the volume of extract subjected to column clean-up.

Fluorodensitometric measurement:

The content in micrograms of aflatoxin B_1 per kg of sample is given by the formula:

$$\frac{S.V}{Y.m}$$

in which:

Y = volume in microlitres of the extract spotted on the platé (10 μl or 20 μl);

S = mass in nanograms of aflatoxin B_1 in the extract spot (proportional to the value of Y taken), deduced from the measurements;

V = final volume of the extract in microlitres, taking into account any dilution that was necessary,

m = mass in grammes of the test portion corresponding to the volume of extract subjected to column clean-up.

Two dimensional TLC procedure (densitometric spotting pattern)

a. **Purpose and scope**

This method makes it possible to determine the level of aflatoxin B_1 in foodstuffs and mixed feeding stuffs, in simple feeding stuffs not falling within the scope of method (a) and in simple feeding stuffs mentioned in the scope of method (a) in which the presence of interfering substances hinders the determination of aflatoxin B_1. It is not applicable to feeding stuffs containing citrus pulp. The lower limit of determination is <u>ca</u> 0.01 mg/kg (10 ppb).

b. **Principle**
(Note: same as in method (a))

c. **Reagents**
(NB: All reagents shall be of "analytical reagent" quality.)

Acetone.

Chloroform, stabilized with 0.5 to 1.0% of ethanol 96% (v/v).

n-Hexane.

Methanol.

Anhydrous diethyl ether, free from peroxides.

Mixture of benzene and acetonitrile: 98/2 (v/v).

Mixture of chloroform and methanol: 97/3 (v/v).

Silica gel, for column chromatography, particle size 0.05 to 0.20 mm.

Absorbent cotton wool, previously defatted with chloroform, or glass wool.

Sodium sulphate, anhydrous, granular.

Inert gas, e.g. nitrogen.

Hydrochloric acid, (1 mol/L).

Diatomaceous earth (Kieselguhr, Hyflosupercel), acid washed.

Silica gel G-HR or equivalent, for selfcoated plates.

Developing solvents:

Mixture of diethyl ether and methanol and water: 94/4.5/1.5 (v/v/v), saturated tank;

Mixture of chloroform and acetone: 9/1 (v/v), unsaturated tank.

Standard solution containing 0.1 μg aflatoxin B_1 per ml in chloroform or the mixture of benzene and acetonitrile, prepared and checked as described below.

Preparation of standard solution and determination of concentration: Proceed as in method (a).

Testing of chromatographic purity of the standard solution:
Proceed as in method (a).

Trifluoroacetic acid (store in tightly closed bottle in refrigerator).

Propanol-2.

Developing solvents for the confirmatory test:

Mixture of chloroform and acetone and methanol: 90/10/2 (v/v/v), unsaturated tank;

Mixture of chloroform and acetone and propanol-2: 85/12.5/2.5 (v/v/v), unsaturated tank.

Sodium hypochlorite (NaOCl), 5% (v/v) solution in water.

d.   **Apparatus**
(Note: same as in method (a))

e.   **Procedure**

Preparation of the test sample: Proceed as in method (a)

Two dimensional thin layer chromatography:

Application of the solutions (follow the diagram in Figure 39).

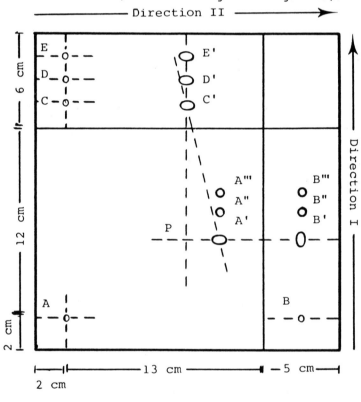

A   : extract of test portion

B,C,D,E and F: aflatoxin B_1 standard

Figure. 39

Inscribe two straight lines on a plate parallel to two contiguous sides (5 and 6 cm from each side respectively), to limit migration of the solvent fronts. Spot the following solutions on the plate using capillary pipettes or the micro-syringe:

- at point A, 20 μl of the extract of the test portion;
- at point B, 20 μl of the standard solution;
- at point C, 10 μl of the standard solution;
- at point D, 20 μl of the standard solution;
- at point E, 40 μl of the standard solution.

Dry in a slow stream of air or inert gas. The spots obtained shall have a diameter of about 5 mm.

Development (follow the diagram in Figure 39)

Develop the plate in direction I, in the dark, using the developing solvent until the solvent front reaches the solvent limit line. Remove the plate from the tank and allow to dry in the dark at ambient temperature for 15 minutes.

Then develop the plate in direction II, in the dark, using the second developing solvent until the solvent front reaches the solvent limit line. Remove the plate from the tank and allow to dry, in the dark, at ambient temperature.

Interpretation of the chromatogram (follow the diagram in Figure 39)

Irradiate the chromatogram with UV light by placing the plate 10 cm from the UV lamp. Locate the position of the blue fluorescent spots B', C', D' and E' of the aflatoxin B_1 from the standard solution. Project two imaginary lines passing through these spots and at right angles to the development directions. The intersection P of these lines is the location in which to expect to find the aflatoxin B_1 spot originating from the extract of the test portion applied at A. However, the actual location of the aflatoxin B_1 spot may be at a point A'; at the intersection of two imaginary straight lines forming an angle of about $100°$ between them and passing through spots B' and C' respectively. Determine the quantity of aflatoxin B_1 in the extract of the test portion.

Supplementary chromatography

Inscribe two straight lines on a new plate parallel to two contiguous sides, as indicated in the diagram in Figure 39 and apply on point A 20 μl of the extract of the test portion and, superimposed on it, 20 μl of the standard solution. Develop as indicated previously. Irradiate the chromatogram with UV light and check that:

- the aflatoxin B_1 spots from the extract and the standard solution are superimposed

- the fluorescence of this spot is more intense than that of the aflatoxin B_1 spot at A' on the first plate.

Determination

Estimate visually or determine by fluorodensitometry as indicated below.

Visual estimation

Estimate the quantity of aflatoxin B_1 in the extract by comparing the intensity of fluorescence of the extract spot (A') with that of the spots C', D' and E' of the standard solution. Interpolate if necessary. If the intensity of fluorescence given by the 20 μl of extract is greater than that of the 40 μl of standard solution, dilute the extract 10 or 100 times with chloroform or the mixture of benzene and acetonitrile before repeating TLC.

Measurement by fluorodensitometry

Measure the intensity of fluorescence of the aflatoxin B_1 spots with the fluorodensitometer at an excitation wavelength of 365 nm and an emission wavelength of 443 nm. Determine the quantity of aflatoxin B_1 in the extract spot (A′) by comparing the intensity of fluorescence of the extract spot with that of spots C′, D′ and E′ of the standard solution. If the intensity of fluorescence given by the 20 μl of extract is greater than that of the 40μl of standard solution, dilute the extract 10 or 100 times with chloroform or the mixture of benzene and acetonitrile before repeating TLC.

Confirmation of the identity of aflatoxin B_1

The first method below is, for practical reasons, preferred because the plate used for quantification is directly suitable for confirmation purposes. In case trifluoroacetic acid is not available, the second method should be used. However, availability of precoated plates and a spray cabinet with suction is then a prerequisite.

Two–dimensional chromatography involving the formation of aflatoxin B_1–hemiacetal (aflatoxin B_{2a}) using trifluoroacetic acid.

Examine the chromatogram under UV light and mark the locations of the spot (B′) (see Figure 39) from the standard solution applied at point B and of the spot (A′) from the extract of the test portion applied at point A of the plate with a soft pencil. Spot with a glass capillary 1–2 μl of trifluoroacetic acid on the spots A′ and B′. Dry with a stream of air at ambient temperature.

Develop the plate again in direction I (see Figure 39), in the dark, using an appropriate developing solvent, until the solvent front reaches the solvent limit line again. Remove the plate from the tank and allow to dry in the dark at ambient temperature for 15 minutes.

Interpretation of the chromatogram (follow the diagram in Figure 39).

Examine the chromatogram under UV light and check for the following features.

(1) Appearance of a weak blue fluorescent spot of unidentified aflatoxin B_1–derivative (position B′′′) and a more intense blue fluorescent spot of aflatoxin B_1–hemiacetal (position B′′) both originating from the standard aflatoxin B_1 (position B′).

(2) Appearance of blue fluorescent spots (positions A′′′ and A′′) originating from the assumed aflatoxin B_1 in the extract (position A′) which R_f–values correspond with both originating from the standard aflatoxin B_1 (position B′). The identity of aflatoxin B_1 in the extract is confirmed when the R_f–values of the aflatoxin B_1–hemiacetal spots from extract and standard (positions A′′ and B′′ respectively) correspond.

Two–dimensional chromatography involving the formation of aflatoxin B_1–hemiacetal (aflatoxin B_{2a}) using hydrochloric acid: Proceed as in method (a). See Figure 37.

f. **Calculation of the results**

Visual estimation

The content in micrograms of aflatoxin B_1 per kg of sample (ppb) is given by the formula:

$$\frac{X.S.V}{Y.m}$$

in which:

X and Y are respectively the volumes in microlitres of the standard solutions of aflatoxin B_1 and of the extract having a similar intensity of fluorescence;

S = mass concentration in micrograms of aflatoxin B_1 per ml of the standard solution;

V = final volume of the extract in microlitres, taking into account any dilution that was necessary;

m = mass in grammes of the test portion corresponding to the volume of extract subjected to column clean-up.

Fluorodensitometric measurement

The content in micrograms of aflatoxin B_1 per kg of sample is given by the formula:

$$\frac{S.V}{Y.m}$$

in which:

Y = volume in microlitres of the extract spotted on the plate (20 μl);

S = mass in nanograms of aflatoxin B_1 in the extract spot proportional to the value of Y taken), deduced from the measurements;

V = final volume of the extract in microlitres, taking into account any dilution that was necessary;

m = mass in grammes of the test portion corresponding to the volume of extract subjected to column clean-up.

Two dimensional TLC procedure (Anti-diagonal spotting pattern)

a. Purpose and scope

The method makes it possible to (visually) determine the level of aflatoxin B_1 in foodstuffs, in simple and in mixed feeding stuffs excluding those containing citrus pulp.

b. Principle

The test portion is subjected to extraction with chloroform. The extract is filtered, and an aliquot portion is taken and purified by column chromatography on silica gel. The eluate is evaporated and the residue redissolved in a specific volume of chloroform or of a mixture of benzene and acetonitrile. An aliquot portion of this solution is subjected to two-dimensional thin layer chromatography (TLC) using the antidiagonal spot application technique in order to pinpoint and facilitate visual comparison between sample and standard B_1 spots. The quantity of aflatoxin B_1 is determined visually under UV irradiation of the chromatogram by comparison with known quantities of standard aflatoxin B_1. The identity of the aflatoxin B_1 extracted from the feeding stuff is confirmed by formation of the hemiacetal of aflatoxin B_1 on the TLC plate.

c. Reagents

(Note: same as in method (b))

d.   **Apparatus**

(Note: same as in method (a))

e.   **Procedure**

Preparation of the test sample:

Proceed as in method (a)

Two-dimensional TLC using the antidiagronal spot application technique

Application of the solutions (follow the diagram in Figure 40)

A   : extract of test portion

B,C,D,E and F: aflatoxin B_1 standard

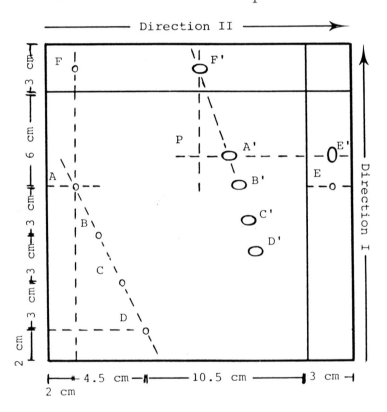

Figure 40

Inscribe two straight lines on a plate parallel to two contiguous sides (3 cm from each side) to limit migration of the solvent fronts. Spot the following solutions on the plate using capillary pipettes or the microsyringe:

- at point A, 20 μl of the extract of the test portion;
- at point B, 10 μl of the standard solution;
- at point C, 20 μl of the standard solution;

- at point D, 40 μl of the standard solution;
- at point E and F, 20 μl of the standard solution.

Dry in a slow stream of air or inert gas. The spots obtained shall have a diameter of about 5 mm.

Development (follow the diagram in Figure 40).

Develop the plate in direction I, in the dark, using the first developing solvent until the solvent front reaches the solvent limit line. Remove the plate from the tank and allow to dry, in the dark, at ambient temperature for 15 minutes.

Then develop the plate in direction II, in the dark, using the second developing solvent until the solvent front reaches the solvent limit line. Remove the plate from the tank and allow to dry, in the dark, at ambient temperature.

Interpretation of the chromatogram (follow the diagram in Figure 40)

Irradiate the chromatogram with uv light by placing the plate 10 cm from the UV-lamp. Locate the position of the blue fluorescent spots B', C', D', E' and F'. Project two imaginary lines passing through spot E' and F' respectively and at right angles to the development directions. The intersection P of these lines is the location in which to expect to find the aflatoxin B_1 spot originating from the extract of the test portion applied at A. However, the actual location of the aflatoxin B_1 spot may be at a point A' at the intersection of an imaginary straight line perpendicular to the direction of the first development through spot E' from starting position E and another imaginary line through the positions B', C' and D' of the standard spots.

Aflatoxin B_1 is present in the test portion if four blue fluorescent spots can be visualized on an imaginary line through the aflatoxin B_1 spots originating from the test portion applied at A and the aflatoxin B_1 standard applied at B, C and D. Determine the quantity of aflatoxin B_1 in the extract of the test portion.

Supplementary chromatography

Inscribe two straight lines on a new plate parallel to two contiguous sides, as indicated in Figure 40, and apply at point A (see Figure 40) 20 μL of the extract of the test portion obtained in 5.3 and superimposed on it, 20 μl of the standard solution. Develop as before. Irradiate the chromatogram with UV light and check that:

- the aflatoxin B_1 spots from the extract and the standard solution are superimposed

- the fluorescence of this spot is more intense than that of the aflatoxin B_1 spot at A' on the first plate.

Determination

Visual estimation

Estimate the quantity of aflatoxin B_1 in the extract by comparing the intensity of fluorescence of the extract spot with the intensities of the three standard B_1 spots located at B', C' and D'. Interpolate if necessary. If the intensity of fluorescence given by the 20 μl of extract is greater than that of the 40 μl of standard solution, dilute the extract 10 or 100 times with chloroform or the mixture of benzene and acetonitrile before repeating TLC.

Confirmation of identity of aflatoxin B_1

Confirm the identity of the aflatoxin B_1 in the extract by the presumptive test with sulphuric acid and, if the result of this test is positive, by the two dimensional TLC confirmation tests. If the result of the presumptive test with sulphuric acid is negative, there is no need to proceed with the actual confirmation since, in this case, no aflatoxin B_1 is present. The second confirmation method is preferred in the case precoated plates and a spray cabinet with suction are available.

Presumptive test with sulphuric acid

Spray sulphuric acid on to the chromatogram. The fluorescence of the aflatoxin B_1 spots shall turn from blue to yellow under UV irradiation.

Two-dimensional chromatography involving the formation of aflatoxin B_1-hemiacetal (aflatoxin B_{2a}) using hydrochloric acid:

Proceed as in Method (a). See Figure 37.

Two-dimensional chromatography involving the formation of aflatoxin B_1-hemiacetal (aflatoxin B_{2a}) using trifluoroacetic acid:

Proceed as in Method (a). See Figure 38.

f.   **Calculation of the results**

Visual estimation

The content in micrograms of aflatoxin B_1 per kg of sample (ppb) is given by the formula:

$$\frac{X.S.V}{Y.m}$$

in which:

X and Y are respectively the volumes in microlitres of the standard solution of aflatoxin B_1 and of the extract having a similar intensity of fluorescence;

S   =   mass concentration in micrograms of aflatoxin B_1 per ml of the standard solution;

V   =   final volume of the extract in microlitres, taking into account any dilution that was necessary;

m   =   mass in grammes of the test portion corresponding to the volume of extract subjected to column clean-up.

Observations concerning TLC procedures

a.   **Defatting**

Samples containing more than 5% fats shall be defatted with light petroleum (bp 40 to 60°C) after the initial preparation.

In such cases, the analytical results shall be expressed in terms of the mass of the non-defatted sample.

b.   **Repeatability of the results**

The difference between the results of two parallel estimations carried out on the sample by the same analyst shall not exceed:

- 25% related to the highest result for contents of aflatoxin B_1 from 10 and up to 20 $\mu g/kg$;

- 5 $\mu g/kg$, for contents greater than 20 and up to 50 $\mu g/kg$;

- 10% related to the highest value for contents above 50 $\mu g/kg$.

c.   **Reproducibility of the results**

The reproducibility of the results, i.e. the variation between the results obtained by two or more laboratories on the same sample has been estimated at:

$\pm$50% of the mean value for mean values of aflatoxin B_1 from 10 and up to 20 $\mu g/kg$;
$\pm$10 $\mu g/kg$ on the mean value for mean values greater than 20 and up to 50 $\mu g/kg$;
$\pm$20% of the mean values above 50 $\mu g/kg$.

d.   **Application of the confirmation procedure with trifluoroacetic acid**

Choice of developing solvents (see the diagram in Figure 38)

A R_f-value of aflatoxin B_1 of 0.5 or less in direction I is desirable in order to have enough space available for the third development after reaction with trifluoroacetic acid.   The R_f-value depends on the type of silica gel used.   In case of a R_f-value higher than 0.5 it is recommended to decrease the methanol-water content of the developing solvent.   Likewise the R_f-value of the aflatoxin B_1-hemiacetal varies with the type of silica gel used.   In order to obtain an optimal migration distance the R_f-value of the aflatoxin B_1-hemiacetal can be adjusted by changing the percentage of methanol in the developing solvent.   A migration distance of the aflatoxin B_1-hemiacetal of 2 cm is considered to be optimal.

Interpretation of the chromatogram (see the diagram in Figure 38)

When low contaminated samples are analysed it is possible that the unidentified aflatoxin B_1-derivative (position A''') cannot be found.   In addition this unidentified aflatoxin B_1-derivative coincides frequently with fluorescing background substances.   The aflatoxin B_1-hemiacetal however is clearly separated and the presence of this spot is primarily used for confirmation.

4.   **Enzyme-linked Immunosorbent Assay for the Determination of Aflatoxin B1 in foods and animal feeds**

Procedure based upon the Agri-Screen[R] method for detection of aflatoxin B1, Neogen Corporation, Lansing MI 48912, USA. Text modified by H.P. van Egmond.

This procedure is one of the various commercial ELISA-test kits that have been developed for the determination of aflatoxins in agricultural commodities. The fact that this procedure is included in this syllabus does not imply approval or recommendation of the Agriscreen test by the Food and Agriculture Organization of the United Nations to the exclusion of other ELISA test procedures which may also be suitable for the determination of aflatoxin B1.

Purpose and scope

The method makes it possible to semi-quantitatively determine aflatoxin B1 in foodstuffs and feedstuffs at levels of ca 20 mcg/kg.   At the time of writing (1987) the full scope of products for which the method is suitable, was yet unknown. Also, the limit(s) of detection could not be given.

Principle

Aflatoxin B1 is conjugated to an enzyme. This conjugate is used as the known antigen (enzyme-conjugate). Antibodies specific to aflatoxin B1 are coated onto plastic microtitre wells. Aflatoxin B1 is extracted from the sample with a solvent. The extract is mixed equally (V/V) with enzyme-conjugated aflatoxin B1 and the mixture is placed in the antibody-coated microtitre wells. The contaminating aflatoxin B1 from the sample, if present, and the enzyme-conjugated aflatoxin B1 compete for the binding sites on the antibody. Unbound aflatoxin B1, from sample and enzyme-conjugate, is "washed" away. A solubilized enzyme substrate is added to each well, and catalyzed by the bound enzyme, if present, from a colourless solution to a blue solution. The intensity of colour decreases as the amount of aflatoxin B1 in the sample increases. After a few minutes the change in colour can be evaluated visually. By adding the red coloured enzyme-stopping reagent, a colour spectrum is created in which light purple to pink or red colour indicates aflatoxin levels above 20 mcg/kg, and a blue to dark blue colour indicates samples with less than 20 mcg/kg of aflatoxin.

Reagents

All but methanol are available in the Agri-Screen^R kit.

Aflatoxin B1 enzyme-conjugate. Lyophilized enzyme-conjugate specific to aflatoxin B1 or equivalent. Do not use beyond expiration date.

Enzyme-conjugate hydration solution. Distilled water.

Antibody-coated solid support. Antibody-coated 12-well microtitre strips or equivalent. Do not use beyond expiration date.

Enzyme-substrate, contains tetramethylbenzidine in citrate buffer (pH 4.0). Stopper after use and store under refrigeration (4°C).

Hydrogen peroxide. Contains 1.5 ml 30% H_2O_2/l in citrate buffer (pH 4.0). Stopper after use and store under refrigeration (4°C).

Colour stopping solution. Contains 3.5 mg HF, 10.5 g sodium citrate, 6 ml NaOH, (c(NaOH) = 1 mol/l) and 400 mg Na4EDTA/l distilled water. Stopper after use and store under refrigeration.

Aflatoxin B1 standards in methanol solution (3.8) Concentrations corresponding to 0, 5, 10, 20, 50 and 100 mcg/kg test sample.

Methanol solution, reagent grade methanol and water: 55/45 (V/V).

Apparatus

The mixing tubes and wells are available in the Agri-Screen^R kit.

Filter paper, Whatman No.1 or equivalent.

Pipettes. Calibrated or automatic pipettor with disposable tips capable of delivering accurate amounts in 0.1-1.0 ml. Eppendorf or equivalent.

Test tubes with screw caps, 50 ml size.

Mixing tubes. Glass or plastic 12 mm x 75 mm with caps.

Mixing wells. 12-well microtitre mixing strip or equivalent. One mixing well per standard or sample to be tested.

Vortex mixer. Capable of vigorous agitation of mixing tubes. S/P mixer (Scientific Products, Inc.) or equivalent.

Procedure

Preparation of the test sample:

Grind the laboratory sample so that it completely passes through a sieve with a 1 mm mesh.

Extraction:

Weigh out 5 g test sample into a test tube with screw cap. Add 25 ml methanol solution, shake vigorously for at least 1 minute. Filter through a filter paper into a 50 ml test tube or equivalent. All samples to be tested should be prepared during the same time period.

Preparation of the enzyme-conjugate working solution:

Add 2 ml enzyme-conjugate hydration solution to the aflatoxin Bl enzyme-conjugate. Mix well to completely dissolve. Do not shake hard enough to cause foaming in the bottle. CAUTION: The working solution must be at room temperature before use and used within 30 minutes after preparation.

Preparation of the enzyme-substrate working solution:

Transfer 1 ml enzyme-substrate and 1 ml hydrogen peroxide to a mixing tube. Close the tube and shake vigorously. CAUTION: The working solution must be used within one hour after preparation.

Enzyme Immuno Assay:

NOTE: A different pipette/tip must be used with each of the following steps. Always pipette into the wells in the same order.

Set up the mixing wells. Do not use the antibody-coated microtitre wells. Pipette 0.1 ml aflatoxin Bl enzyme-conjugate working solution into each well. Use one well for each sample to be tested and one well for each control. Up to six aflatoxin Bl control wells can be used with each strip. Add 0.1 ml aflatoxin Bl of the standard solutions and sample filtrate into the separate wells and mix thoroughly by drawing the fluid back into the pipette/tip. Change the pipette/tip between each sample and control.

Set up the antibody-coated wells. Transfer 0.1 ml of the solution from each mixing well to the corresponding antibody-coated well. Change the pipettes/tips between each transfer. Let stand at ambient temperature (22 - 25°C) for 10 minutes.

Shake the solution out of the antibody-coated wells into the waste receptacle containing decontaminating solution (See Safety Note (7)). Do not get decontaminating solution into the wells. Wash the wells 10 times by filling with distilled water and shaking out the wash solution. After the final wash, invert the wells on absorbent paper and tap to remove excess water.

NOTE: Only one pipette tip need to be used for each of the following steps:

Preparation of the enzyme-conjugate working solution:

Immediately add 0.1 ml enzyme-substrate working solution to each antibody-coated well and let stand at ambient temperature for 5 minutes. Gently agitate the well several times during the assay by holding on the countertop and tapping on the side.

Add 0.1 ml colour stopping solution to each antibody well and compare the colour development of the control wells with the sample wells. Hold the strips against a white background for comparison.

Interpretation of results

Compare the colour of each sample well to the standards in that strip. Report the concentration of the sample based on the standard it most closely resembles. The colour of the 20 mcg/kg aflatoxin B1 standard usually is light purple. If a sample's colour is bluer than the 20 mcg/kg aflatoxin B1 standard, the sample contains less than 20 mcg/kg. If a sample's colour is more pink or red than the 20 mcg/kg standard, the sample contains more than 20 mcg/kg. Depending upon the operator the standard may be light purple to lavender to slightly pink, but the interpretation of the sample will remain the same.

Safety notes

Soak all used laboratory ware, pipette tips and kit components in a 10% solution of household bleach before discard ing (Household bleach generally contains 5.25% sodium hypochlorite).

V LECTURES

1. Mycotoxins: introduction

Mycotoxins are secondary metabolites of fungi which may produce toxic, carcinogenic, mutagenic, teratogenic and oestrogenic properties. The term "mycotoxin" is derived from the Greek words "MYKES" (fungus) and "TOKSIKON" (poison) (1). The toxicity syndromes resulting from the intake of mycotoxins by man and animals are named "mycotoxicoses". Although some fungi, such as the ergot-producing Claviceps purpurea have been known for centuries because of their high and acute toxicity, it was only after the discovery of the aflatoxins in 1960 in the United Kingdom, that research showed that a large number of other fungus species could form other and equally important toxic secondary metabolites. Three different ideas exist about the possible function of secondary metabolites (2). One hypothesis claims that the formation of secondary metabolites keeps the mould active when the substrate is exhausted; another claims that the formation of metabolites prevents the accumulation of abnormal, possibly harmful compounds; and a third hypothesis is that secondary metabolism has a selective value in ecological systems: mycotoxins might be produced as a self-defense mechanism against other organisms as some of the mycotoxins are toxic to higher animals, insects and micro-organisms. It has been shown that pure-culturing in laboratory circumstances often leads to disappearance of the mycotoxin-producing potency, which could be explained by the absence of natural enemies. However it is most likely due to mutation or selection of poor toxin producing strains, because of the medium. In fact, it is doubtful that the mould needs to produce mycotoxins because both toxic and non-toxic species could occur in nature to some degree.

Mycotoxicoses have been known for a long time. The first recognized mycotoxicosis was problably ergotism, a disease, characterized by necrosis and gangrene and better known in the Middle Ages in Europe under the name "Holy fire", which was caused by the intake of grain contaminated with sclerotia of Claviceps purpurea. Despite the fact that mycotoxins were known for a long time mycotoxicoses were the "NEGLECTED DISEASES" until the early 1960's (3). Then this attitude changed drastically by the outbreak of TURKEY-X DISEASE in Great Britain. Within a few months more than 100.000 turkeys died. The appearance of Turkey-X disease led to a multidisciplinary approach to investigate the cause of the problem. These efforts were successful and the cause of the disease was traced to a toxic factor occurring in the Brazilian groundnut meal which was used as a protein source in the feed of those affected poultry. The toxic factor seemed to be produced by two fungi, A. parasiticus and A. flavus and hence, the name "AFLATOXIN" was given to it, an acronym derived from the name of the second mentioned fungus (4). Further study of the toxic factor demonstrated that the material could be separated chromatographically into four distinct spots (5). These four components have been named aflatoxins B1,B2,G1 and G2 according to their colour of fluorescence and their relative chromatographic mobility. Later on it became clear that the group of aflatoxins consists of at least 17 closely related compounds, some of which may occur in animal products by the carry-over of mycotoxins occurring in animal feedstuff ingested by cattle. The aflatoxins are very dangerous for humans and animals, not only because of their acute toxicity in high doses, but especially because of their strong carcinogenic properties. Epidemiological evidence points to a higher incidence of liver tumors in people who regularly eat food contaminated with aflatoxins.

In the two decades following the outbreak of Turkey-X disease, a wealth of information about aflatoxins has been produced and, in addition, it became clear that a large number of fungal species could form mycotoxins. At present over 200 different mycotoxins are known, showing a large variety of chemical structures. Examples of a few of these structures are shown in the slide (6). Aflatoxin B1 is the most notorious mycotoxin, with a characteristic difuran moiety and a lactone ring. Both parts of the molecule are suspected to play a role in its carcinogenicity. Ochratoxin A is another well-known mycotoxin, which has a peptide bond and a Cl-atom in its molecular structure. The latter seems to be rather peculiar for natural products. Ochratoxin A causes kidney damage. In Europe several areas occur where nephropathy is observed among man and animals, a renal disease which is possibly associated with the intake of ochratoxin A with the food. Patulin is a rather small molecule, it has a lactone ring as aflatoxin B1 and ochratoxin A. Patulin has been used in the past as an antibiotic, nowadays it is considered a mycotoxin, which may be produced on fruits and which causes haemorrhages and oedema in experimental animals. Lysergic acid is a building stone of the ergot-alkaloids which caused ergotism in the Middle Ages as mentioned before. The last structure is that of a more complicated mycotoxin, T-2 toxin, which has an epoxy-group, a characteristic from the thrichothecenes, produced by certain Fusarium strains. For the African countries, the aflatoxins are probably the most important mycotoxins.

Humans may be exposed to mycotoxins not only through ingestion of toxin-contaminated food, but also by inhalation or skin contact (7). An example of human exposure through inhalation is the observation of Van Nieuwenhuize, who reported the development of cancers in various organs of workers who had been inhaling small dust particles loaded with aflatoxins for several years in an oil-mill crushing peanuts and other oil seeds.

The most important route however, is the exposure by contaminated food. Food raw materials and products can be contaminated with spores of conidia and mycelium fragments from the environment. Contamination can occur at different stages of production: during growth and ripening of the crops, during processing of semi-completed products and in consumer products. The presence of potential toxinogenic species on food products does not always mean that these products contain mycotoxins, because the environmental conditions for fungal growth are not necessarily the same as those for toxin production, as will be shown in one of the coming slides.

On the other hand, the presence of mycotoxins, does not always mean that the products in question are moulded. Through heat treatment of contaminated products (e.g. roasting of peanuts and pelleting of feedstuffs), the mould count can be drastically reduced, whereas many mycotoxins are heat-stable. Also carry-over of mycotoxins may occur from feedstuffs to animal products such as meat, milk and eggs. These animal products then may contain mycotoxins, without being moulded. Much scientific attention has been paid to dairy product contamination as it was found that aflatoxin B1, the most notorious of the mycotoxins, is converted by the dairy cow into its 4-hydroxy derivative, aflatoxin M1 (8), which appears in the milk. Experiments with cows have shown that about 1-4% of the ingested aflatoxin B1 can be recovered in the milk as aflatoxin M1. It is uncertain whether M1 has carcinogenic properties. Limited carcinogenicity studies with rainbow trout and recently with rats revealed that M1 is much less carcinogenic than aflatoxin B1. However no extensive studies on the carcinogenicity of aflatoxin M1 are published, probably because of the lack of sufficient pure material has precluded such studies. Because of its high toxicity and the uncertainty concerning its possible carcinogenicity, presence of this compound is considered to be undesirable in food. In consequence a number of countries has enacted legal measures to control M1 contamination in milk and milk products.

For developing countries the direct contamination of agricultural commodities with mycotoxins is more important then the indirect way by carry-over.

Fungal growth only occurs under favourable conditions. Fungi need various nutrients to meet their energy needs and to form macromolecules such as proteins and DNA. Many of the foodstuffs for human and animal consumption contain the necessary nutrients and can therefore serve as substrate. A large number of metabolites are formed during the breakdown of carbohydrates, some of which can accumulate under certain conditions, for instance ethanol and organic acids. During and especially at the end of the growth period, certain metabolites are synthesized, which obviously are not necessary for the growth and energy supply of the mould. Some of these secondary metabolites are toxic for micro-organisms and these are referred to as antibiotics. Others are (also) toxic for higher animals, these are named mycotoxins.

In addition to the presence of nutrients, the most important factors for growth and mycotoxin production are temperature (9) and water activity. The optimal temperatures (10) for growth of most Penicillia is at 25-30°C and for Aspergilli at 30-40°C, temperatures that will be often met in developing countries Fusarium species can be regarded as psychrophilic, because of their low optimal temperature of 8-15°C, and these species occur in the moderate climates.

The factor water activity (aW) is a measure for the unbound water in the food which is available for the growth of the mould. This term is explained in the slide (11). The relative humidity is used for the atmosphere, the equilibrium relative humidity or the equilibrium relative water vapour pressure is in equilibrium with the humidity of the stored material. The water activity is (12). The more water is bound to the substrate, the less water is available to the fungus and the lower the aW. The aW not only influences fungal growth but it also affects the production of mycotoxins. Below certain aW values, mycotoxins are not produced. These values depend on the mycotoxin concerned, the fungal strain involved, the substrate and the temperature.

In the slide (13) the a range for growth of Aspergillus flavus and aflatoxin production on malt extract sucrose agar at various temperatures is shown. The rate of fungal growth is represented by the open columns, whereas the amount of aflatoxin B1 produced is represented by the white columns. The aW for aflatoxin production ranges from 0.87 to 1.00 and the temperature ranges from 12 to 37°C. Furthermore, the optimum aW for toxin production which is 0.99 is higher than for growth, which is 0.95. The minimal aW values for fungal growth and toxin production may differ for the various substrates, and the Codex Alimentarius Committee on Food Hygiene has proposed an aW standard of 0.70 for peanuts to prevent contamination with aflatoxins.

For measuring the aW of a substrate a rather complicated measuring system is ordinarily necessary. However Northolt developed a simple screening technique for estimating the a of foodstuffs, the so-called salt crystal liquefaction test. This test is based on the property of salt crystals to attract water vapour and to liquefy if the water vapour pressure of the surrounding air exceeds the water vapour pressure of the saturated solution of the salt. About 40-80 g of sample, for instance peanuts are placed in a jar (14), which is then closed and equilibrated for at least two hours. Then the jar is opened briefly (15) and a very thin layer of vaseline is sprayed on the inner surface of the lid. A few dozens of the appropriate crystals—in this case $CuCl_2.2H_2O$—are strewed on the vaseline with the help of a spatula. The jar is closed and equilibrated for about 4 hours. Then, the crystals are observed to see whether they are liquefied or not (16). When 50% or more of the crystals are liquefied, the test result is regarded to be positive, which means the aW of the sample > specific aW of the salt. In this example $CuCl_2.2H_2O$ crystals were used, which have a specific aW= 0.70. This means that the aW of the peanuts > 0.70 and, hence, the sample shown in the slide does not comply with the proposed Codex Standard for peanuts. The salt crystal liquefaction test can be easily applied in the field and it takes a few hours before obtaining the result. The salt crystal liquefaction test is an indirect physical field test that indicates only the possibility that a mycotoxin is present. Direct evidence can be obtained by applying methods of analysis to determine the actual presence of one or more mycotoxins in the commodity to be inspected.

There are two approaches possible for the detection and determination of mycotoxins: biological and chemical. Biological methods may be useful in screening for known and unknown mycotoxins. As an example, they have played a role of importance in the period of the discovery of the aflatoxins. However, bio-assays generally lack specificity and reproducibility, and chemical assays are to be preferred for the determination of mycotoxins contain the basic steps as outlined in the next slide (17).

Sampling is an integral part of the analysis procedure. The object of the sampling procedure is to obtain a laboratory sample (test portion) representative of the lot from which it is drawn. The decision whether to accept or reject a lot will be based on the evidence gained from analysis of the sample. Sampling can pose an immense problem, for instance if the toxin is distributed inhomogeneously through the lot to be inspected. Bags with peanuts (18) may include a few aflatoxin-containing nuts unequally distributed between the good nuts. The next slide (19) illustrates the results of the analysis of 10 subsamples drawn from one lot. The mean concentration of aflatoxin B1 was found to be 36 mcg/kg, whereas the results ranged from 0-165 mcg/kg. This example clearly illustrates the difficulties encountered when asked to approve or reject the lot on the basis of a few analyses. Statisticians still disagree about which sampling procedure should be used to obtain the best estimation of actual toxin content. In spite of these problems sampling procedures have been made for some commodities. An example is the sampling method for feedstuffs which is officially used in the European Communities (EC) (20).

The actual analysis of the test portion (usually 20–100 g) starts with isolation of the component of interest. Generally, mycotoxins are extracted with an organic solvent such as chloroform, dichloromethane, acetonitrile, ethylacetate, acetone and methanol (21). These solvents may be used in combination with small amounts of water and acids. Since mycotoxins are normally only present in very low amounts, a strong concentration of the extract is necessary to make final detection possible. The frequent presence of lipids and other components hamper adequate concentration and final detection. In these cases the samples must be purified prior to concentration. Several column chromatographic clean-up steps are possible with materials such as silica gel, aluminium oxide, polyamid, Florisil and Sephadex (22). Silica gel is most frequently used. The final choice of the column material depends on the substances to be eliminated (matrix compounds) and the component of interest, which is the mycotoxin to be determined. After addition of the extract to the clean-up column, impurities are usually washed off with solvents in which the toxins are insoluble or less soluble than the impurities. Then the solvent composition is changed in such a way that the toxins are selectively eluted from the column and the eluate is collected. In some procedures liquid-liquid extraction is carried out in separating funnels, for instance pentane with methanol-water. Since most toxins are not lipophilic, fats can be removed in this way without toxin.

All these purification techniques are in fact separation procedures in which groups of substances with different physico-chemical behaviour are separated from one another. In this way the greater part of the co-extractives can be removed, without toxin. Extracts that have been cleaned-up are usually concentrated by evaporating the solvent with a rotary evaporator or by using a steam bath. After concentration a so-called final extract is obtained, which is then further submittted to the determinative step. Despite the clean-up procedure applied, the final extract may contain other co-extracted substances, which may interfere with the mycotoxin determination. Several possibilities exist to separate the mycotoxin of interest from these matrix-components. Chromatographic procedures, which are physical separation techniques are most often used (23). For developing countries one- and two-dimensional thin layer chromatography (TLC) must be considered as the most important of the chromato graphic techniques for the determination of mycotoxins and there fore a separate lecture is devoted to these techniques.

Methods based on quite different principles than the chromatographic methods are the immuno assays (24). The immuno assays are still in an early stage of application for mycotoxin research. However, especially Enzyme-linked Immunosorbent Assay (ELISA) is rapidly gaining ground and therefore a separate lecture (V3) is devoted to ELISA techniques.

Slide (1)   Explanation of term "mycotoxin"
      (2)   Possible functions of mycotoxins
      (3)   Mycotoxicoses: Neglected diseases
      (4)   A flavus toxin: aflatoxin
      (5)   Picture of aflatoxin spots on TLC plate
      (6)   Structures of some important mycotoxins
      (7)   Routes of exposure to mycotoxins
      (8)   Chemical structures of aflatoxins B1 and M1
      (9)   Main factors for fungal growth and toxin production
     (10)   Optimal temperatures for growth of Penicillium,
                  Aspergillus and Fusarium
     (11)   Different parameters related to water vapour
     (12)   Definition of aW
     (13)   aW and temperature range for growth of A. flavus
                  and aflatoxin production
     (14)   Salt crystal liquefaction test: step 1
     (15)   Salt crystal liquefaction test: step 2
     (16)   Salt crystal liquefaction test: step 3
     (17)   Basic steps of analytical procedures
     (18)   Storage of peanut bags in Nigeria
     (19)   Inhomogeneous distribution of aflatoxin in
                  peanuts in a lot

2. Thin-layer chromatographic techniques

"Chromatography implements an ancient principle –DIVIDE AND RULE– substances are subjected to division resulting in man's rule over the elements. Rule in the name of good, for the benefit of mankind. Although it was discovered 75 years ago, chromatography keeps on developing and continues to remain forever young and fruitful".

These words of Dr. Chmutov, Chairman of the Scientific Council of Sciences of the USSR were addressed in the late 1970's to those who were receiving the "Tswett" Gold Medal on the occasion of the 75th anniversary of Tswett's discovery of chromatography. This commemorative medal is without doubt, the highest award made for outstanding achievements in the development of chromatography. Tswett was a Russian botanist who succeeded in separating the carotenes and several xanthophylls present in organic extracts of green leaves by passing the organic solution through a column of solid adsorbent, such as calcium carbonate. Several coloured plant pigments became visible and so the process became known as "chromatography", after the Greek words **khroma** and **graphein**, meaning "colour" and "to write". In his doctoral dissertation (1) Tswett gave a more detailed description of the process. He recognized the process as an adsorption phenomenon. The least strongly adsorbed pigments were washed through the column rapidly, whereas more strongly adsorbed pigments were immobilized by their adsorption, so their migration rate through the column was greatly reduced.

Besides "adsorption chromatography", where the separation is based on the different adsorption affinities of the sample components toward the surface of an active solid, the following types of chromatography can be identified (2): partition chromatography, ion-exchange chromatography, exclusion chromatography, ion-pair chromatography and affinity chromatography. Of these only adsorption and partition chromatography are of importance in the analysis for mycotoxins. As the other mechanisms of separation are of minor importance, they will not be further discussed here. There are very few examples of pure adsorption chromatography (e.g. working with carbo medicinals) and of pure partition chromatography (e.g. paper chromatography). For most of the time the phenomenon on which the separation is based is a combination of adsorption and partition chromatography. This type of chromatography can be subdivided (3) into:

a. Gravity-flow liquid chromatography (of which Tswett's column was the first application).

b. High performance liquid chromatography (a recent technique in which high inlet pressures and small diameter particles are used).

c. Thin-layer chromatography, whose characteristics and possible application to the determination of mycotoxins will be discussed now.

Thin layer chromatography (TLC) is also a fairly "recent" separation technique. Although the principles of TLC were described before World War II by Izmailow (1938), the technique was most widely applied in the sixties when E. Stahl "rediscovered" TLC. His greatest merit was the standardization of the adsorbents then available. Thin layer chromatography can be defined (4) as "Separation of small amounts of mixtures into zones on a thin layer of adsorbent". The thin layer (stationary phase) is fixed to a carrierplate, e.g. glass or metal, mainly by spreading a suspension of sorbent to which a binder has been added. After drying and conditioning such a thin layer plate, a small volume of the sample extract to be separated is applied onto the plate, which is then placed, usually vertically, in a separation chamber (often called the tank) partially filled with the mobile phase, the so-called developing solvent. This developing solvent migrates through the thin layer because of capillary forces. Depending on their physico-chemical characteristics, the extract components move to a greater or lesser extent with the mobile phase and separated fractions appear as spots behind the mobile phase front on the layer. If the separation is carried out in one direction only, the term one-dimensional TLC is used (5). If that separation is not satisfactory, another development may be carried out in a direction at right angles to the first one, using another type of developing solvent (6). In this case the term two-dimensional TLC is used.

The displacement of the separated substances can be expressed by their rate of flow, usually abbreviated as Rt-value, which can be defined as (7): Distance of migration of compound/Distance of migration of solvent. The Rt-value is always smaller than unity, and, by convention, it is usually quoted to two decimal places. For a given solvent/ adsorbent system Rt-values are characteristic and reproducible for each compound. The parameters adsorbent (stationary phase), solvent (mobile phase) and the compound to be chromatographed, form the three basic parts of a chromatographic system. Variations in stationary phase and/or mobile phase result in changes in Rt-values of solutes and therefore offer the possibility of separating the solute of interest (i.e. the mycotoxin to be assayed) from others thus making detection and determination possible.

In thin layer chromatography a wide range of adsorbents can be used. For mycotoxin research silica gel TLC plates are most often used as this type of adsorbent generally offers the best possibility of separating the toxin of interest from matrix components. Silicagel TLC plates can be made in the laboratory, using the proper equipment (8). They can also be obtained as precoated plates from several commercial firms. The characteristics of precoated as well as selfcoated plates may differ from brand to brand and even from batch to batch, leading to different separation behaviour, as shown in the slide (9), where a mixture of aflatoxins B1, B2, G1 and G2 has been separated on three different types of plates.

Both precoated and selfcoated plates offer advantages. Selfcoated plates (10) allow a free selection of adsorbent and a free selection of additives (e.g. calcium sulphate as a binder of the silicagel to the glass plate, EDTA as a complexing agent, pH regulating agents like oxalid acid). The thickness of the thin layer of selfcoated plates may be varied by adjusting the outlet of the spreader. Finally, selfcoated plates are less expensive then precoated plates. Precoated plates, on the other hand (11), generally possess more uniform and rigid layers and do permit a certain choice of support, e.g. glass, plastic or aluminium. They are ready to use and can be simply stored in their original packing boxes, even when these are open for a longer period of time. Selfcoated plates, however, need drying and activation at ca. 110°C, after which the plates should be kept in a desiccator until use. For proper storage (12) special drying racks are available, designed in such a way, that they fit into a desiccator and so that the plates can be inserted horizontally without damaging the thin layer. Storage of the plates after their development can be done in simple wooden boxes which protect the plates from light, atmospheric influences and mechanical damage.

TLC may not only be used to separate substances and to identify them by Rt-values, it may also be used to quantify the analyte present in the mixture.

The accuracy of the results obtained in quantitative TLC depends to a considerable extent upon the precision with which material can be applied to the plates. In the TLC analysis of mycotoxins, the material that is applied to the plate generally has a volume in the range 5-25 mcl. Depending on the desired accuracy (a measure for the systematic error) and precision (a measure for the accidental error) (13) different types of applicators (14) are used. For screening purposes the disposable qualitative capillary pipettes will satisfy. For quantitative work disposable quantitative capillary pipettes or precision syringes, which are more accurate and precise, are used. Moreover the latter allow the intermittant application of larger volumes under inert atmosphere by using them in combination with a repeating dispenser built-in in a spotting device (15). Spotting devices can be self-made or obtained commercially.

The spotting solvent, which should be the same for the extract and standard, must allow (16) good solubility of the toxin of interest, be volatile and lead to small and uniform spots. These requirements are of major importance in obtaining reproducible results.

TLC plates can be used in different formats (17). Most separation problems may be resolved using a square 20x20 cm plate; however the use of 10x10 cm plates will often lead to good results and even 7x7 cm self-cut plates are useful, especially for rapid screening procedures. The smaller plate sizes addition ally offer the possibility of developing the plates not only in especially designed developing chambers, but also in simple beakers or in series of 10 at a time in a so-called multiplate rack thus significantly reducing the overall time required for a series of TLC runs.

The solvent system employed must obviously afford adequate separation of the components of the mixture to be assayed. The solvent system generally consists of two or more solvents of different polarity, because the use of mixtures generally results in better separations than with single component solvents. To be sure that reproducible results are obtained, analytical grade solvents should be used. As a general rule for TLC on silica gel plates, an increase of the polarity of the developing solvent leads to an increase of the Rt-values. The optimal Rt-values of compounds of interest are considered to be between 0.25 and 0.75. The separation between different components of the mixture to be assayed can be influenced by changing the ratio of the various solvents of the solvent system or by adding or deleting such a compositional solvent.

Other factors may also be important here, such as the type and size of the separation chamber used and the extent of saturation of such a chamber with solvent vapour(s). Saturation of a tank with solvent vapour leads to lower and often more consistent Rt-values. This is because the extent of migration of substances depends on the rate of flow of the developing solvent. In tanks saturated with vapour this solvent flow is much less and much more equable over the plate. A practical advantage is that the running times are hereby shortened. The simplest way of saturating a tank is lining it inside completely with filter paper, and filling the tank with the developing solvent to saturate the paper with the developing solvent.

The spotting of sample and standard(s) is normally carried out according to a spotting pattern, prescribed as a part of the whole analysis procedure. Such a spotting pattern can be a pattern for one-dimensional TLC or, in the case of "dirty" extract, one for two-dimensional TLC.

An example (18) of a spotting pattern for one-dimensional TLC is that of the CB-procedure, which can be applied for the determination of aflatoxin B1 in peanuts, peanut products and corn. Small amounts of sample-extract and B1 standard are spotted onto a 20x20 cm plate, at an imaginary line 4 cm from the bottom edge of the TLC plate. On top of one of the sample spots 5 mcl of the B1 standard is spotted as an internal standard. 5 mcl of a qualitative aflatoxins standard mixture is also spotted to show whether adequate resolution is attained. The TLC plate leaves enough space to spot other sample extracts in which the B1 content can be estimated with the same series of standards. After evaporation of the spotting solvent the plate is placed in a developing tank with a mixture of chloroform and acetone (9+1) and the plate is developed until the solvent reaches the solvent limit line (a line drawn at 16 cm from the bottom edge of the plate), a process which takes approximately 40 minutes. After drying, the plate is observed under long wave U.V. light in order to make visualization and quantification of the aflatoxin spots possible (19). At the left hand side of the plate the result of the separation of an extract of raw peanuts, contaminated with aflatoxin B1 and obtained following the CB-procedure, is visible. From the separation of the aflatoxin standard mixture it may be concluded that the separation quality of the plate has been sufficient. With the help of the B1 standards the B1 spot in the extract can be located and its quantity estimated, so that the initial concentration of the sample can be calculated. It is much more difficult to locate and quantify the B1 present in peanut butter. Because of the roasting process many components have been formed which may seriously hamper the interpretation and quantification of the TLC result. In order to improve the separation in this case, and thus to lower the limit of detection, two dimensional TLC has to be used.

Depending on the way quantitation is carried out, i.e. by densitometry or by visual estimation, the spotting pattern for standards and sample has to be adapted. If a densitometer is used, the densitometric spotting pattern is used. For visual estimation the anti-diagonal spotting pattern is often to be preferred to the densitometric spotting pattern.

In the densitometric spotting pattern (20) an aliquot of sample (extract of peanut butter) is spotted at A and known amounts of B1 standard are spotted at B. The plate is then developed in the first direction and, after drying, the plate is turned 90 degrees and developed in the second direction. Detection and quantification is carried out under U.V.-light (21) with the help of the co-developed B1 standards, the well-separated B1 spot from the sample can be located. By means of a densitometer or TLC-scanner the intensities of fluorescence of the B1 spot from sample and standard can be compared and thus the B1 concentration in the initial sample can be calculated.

If a densitometer is not available the anti-diagonal spotting pattern is to be preferred (22). An aliquot of sample (peanut butter) is spotted at A and different amounts of B1 standard are spotted at the points B. The plate is developed two dimensionally, and detection and quantification are again carried out under U.V.-light (23). With the help of the row of two dimensionally developed B1 standards, B1 from the extract can be located and its concentration estimated by comparing its intensity of fluorescence with that of the different B1 standards. As all the B1 spots are in a line and rather close to each other, such an estimation is easier than visual comparison with standard spots developed in the side lanes, as in the case in the densitometric spotting pattern.

The choice whether to apply one- or two-dimensional TLC depends on the quality of the final extract and on the desired limit of detection (24). Advantages of the one-dimensional variant are rapidness, simplicity and economy, but the resolution obtained is generally limited and intensive clean-up procedures may be required. Two-dimensional TLC on the other hand requires much more time and material and is less easily to apply, but resolution is dramatically improved without intensifying the clean-up procedures. The pros and cons of both variants of TLC should be considered in relation to the requirements of a specific analysis-problem.

The way mycotoxins are detected depends on the physico-chemical properties of the mycotoxin involved. Aflatoxins strongly absorb U.V.-light and emit the energy of the absorbed U.V.-light as fluorescence light. Fortunately this characteristic enables the analyst to detect these components, as demonstrated in the thin layer chromatogram of peanuts and peanut butter. Unfortunately, not all mycotoxins can be detected by such a simple method. Many do not fluoresce under U.V.-light, some show U.V or visible light absorption, while others do not (25). In the latter case they can sometimes be made visible by derivatization, for instance by spraying a reagent on the plate or by exposing the plate to reagent vapour.

One example of a spraying technique is that, commonly used for visualization of sterigmatocystin, a toxin sometimes occurring in grains and in cheese. Two thin layer plates are shown (26) with developed sterigmatocystin spots of increasing concentration. The TLC plate at the right hand side is sprayed with a solution of AlCl in ethanol. Both plates are irradiated with U.V.-light, only the spots on the plate with AlCl solution are visible as yellow fluorescent spots. The use of this spraying reagent improves the limit of detection by a factor of 100.

In spite of all clean-up techniques used, there are still substances which behave in the same manner as the mycotoxin being estimated in TLC separation. In order to minimize the possibility of false-positives, the identity of the mycotoxin in positive samples has to be confirmed. The most reliable method for this purpose is high resolution mass spectroscopy (MS). MS in combination with TLC however is rather time-consuming and not every laboratory is equipped with this sophisticated type of apparatus. Therefore simple chemical techniques have to be applied. Such techniques do not offer the same absolute certainty as MS, but they do exclude nearly all false-positives. Sometimes it is possible to carry out such confirmatory tests directly on TLC plates, thus using the advantages of TLC.

An example of such a test for the confirmation of aflatoxin B1 in extracts of food and feed is the separation – reaction – separation test with hydrochloric acid as developed by Verhülsdonk. This test can even be applied to very "dirty" extracts such as from rabbit feeding stuff. Sample and standard are spotted on a TLC plate (27) in the usual way as for two dimensional TLC. Separation is first made in one direction after which hydrochloric acid is sprayed on the shaded area. After reaction separation is carried out in the second dimension, under exactly identical conditions. The reaction of hydrochloric acid with aflatoxin B1, which has already been separated in the first run, leads to the formation of a hemiacetal B1, which has a specific R-value, lower than that of B1. This is recognized after subsequent chromatography in second direction. Other components must lie on a diagonal line bisecting the plate, as the separation was carried out in both directions under exactly identical conditions. In the slide (28) the result of such a confirmation test for rabbit feedstuff is demonstrated.

The points of importance in TLC can be summarized in 10 basic steps (29): First the analyst should define his problem: Which is the toxin of interest, what matrix is involved, and what should be the limit of detection? Once the problem is defined, a choice has to be made from the list of possible adsorbents which can be used. For mycotoxins SiO will normally be the adsorbent of choice. The format of the plate will depend on the requirements the analyst has concerning separation, precision and rapidity of the method. The choice of developing solvent(s) depends on the physicochemical characteristics of the toxin of interest. As a matter of routine satisfactory separations should be achieved with the R-values of the solute laying between 0.25-0.75. Sample and standard may be applied to the plate by capillary pipettes of syringes. The former are disposable, the latter are more accurate and precise but should be intensively cleaned to prevent cross contamination. Spots should be kept as small as possible and equally sized. Standardization of development conditions is a prerequisite for reproducible results. Visualization of the toxin spots depends on their physico-chemical characteristics. Some toxins absorp visible or U.V.-light, others fluoresce after irradiation with U.V.-light and sometimes spraying or vapourizing with reagents is necessary. Identification occurs with the help of co-developed standards and estimation may be achieved visually or by densitometry. If a sample is considered to be positive, a test should be carried out to confirm its identity, preferably by carrying out a reaction leading to a reaction product with specific TLC characteristics.

Finally a warning to chose using densitometers to measure intensities of spots on TLC plates. Although such TLC scanners offer attractive possibilities and serious advantages, facilitate the estimation, and lead to more precise estimation, one should bear in mind that a small mistake in handling such a piece of apparatus or a small defect in it may lead to figures that have no validity. Though practical, densitometers are not a must. It is a good laboratory practice to always start assessment of a plate by visual estimation. It has been said before in other connections, and it is equally true here (30): "It is better to be approximately right than precisely wrong"!

Slide	(1)	= Picture of frontpage of dissertation of Tswett
	(2)	= Scheme of mechanisms in chromatography
	(3)	= Scheme of subdivision of adsorption chromatography
	(4)	= Definition of TLC
	(5)	= Picture of one-dimensional separation of dyes
	(6)	= Picture of two-dimensional separation of dyes
	(7)	= Definition of R-value
	(8)	= Picture of necessary equipment for self preparation of TLC plates
	(9)	= Picture of separation of aflatoxins standard mixture on several types of SiO TLC plates
	(10)	= Advantages of selfcoated plates
	(11)	= Advantages of precoated plates
	(12)	= Picture of TLC plate rack and TLC plate storage box
	(13)	= Description of accuracy and precision
	(14)	= Picture of various kinds of spotting TLC applicators

    (15)   = Picture of home-made spotting device
    (16)   = Requirements for spotting solvents
    (17)   = Picture of usual plate formats with their respective
                developing chambers
    (18)   = Scheme of the spotting pattern of the CB-method
    (19)   = Picture of the separation of extracts of raw peanuts
                and peanutbutter according to the CB-procedure
    (20)   = Scheme of the spotting pattern for two-dimensional TLC
                (densitometric quantification)
    (21)   = Picture of the separation of an extract of peanut butter submitted
                to two-dimensional TLC, using the densitometric spotting
                pattern
    (22)   = Scheme of the anti-diagonal spotting pattern for two-dimensional TLC
    (23)   = Picture of the separation of an extract of peanut butter submitted
                to two-dimensional TLC using the anti-diagonal spotting pattern
    (24)   = Advantages and disadvantages of one- and two-dimensional TLC
    (25)   = Visualization aids in TLC of mycotoxins
    (26)   = Picture of sterigmatocystin spots visualized and non-visualized
                with AlCl reagent
    (27)   = Schematic presentation of the confirmatory test with HCl
    (28)   = Picture of the result of the HCl confirmatory test applied on
                aflatoxin B1 contaminated rabbit feed
    (29)   = Ten basic steps in TLC
    (30)   = "It is better to be approximately right than
                precisely wrong!"

3. ELISA techniques

Already in ancient times man was fascinated by the protection that may be obtained
against a certain disease after going through the process of that disease. It was not
until around 1900, when it was discovered that protecting factors in the blood appeared as
a response to the invading organisms or substances. The invaders able to evoke specific
reactions against themselves, were called "antigens", the produced protecting factors were
called "antibodies" (1). Later it became clear that antibodies are in vivo produced
proteins (immunoglobulins) which selectively bind with the corresponding antigens. It was
discovered that these immunological reactions had a chemical basis and that they could
occur not only in vivo but in vitro as well.

On the basis of this knowledge immunochemical methods of analysis or "immuno assays"
could be developed. In these assays the molecular recognition properties of the antibodies
are used, rather as a lock responds to a key (2). The key to be measured is the antigen.

Before using immunochemical methods for the detection and quantification of a
constituant (the antigen), the biological reagents involved in these methods (the
antibodies) have to be prepared in higher animals by immunizing them with the antigen. Not
all antigens have the capacity of inducing the formation of antibodies in test animals.
The immunogenicity depends to some extent on the size of the antigen. Small molecules,
like mycotoxins, are not immunogenic; they are called haptens (3). Once the hapten is
bound to a large carrier, which is generally a protein, it becomes immunogenic. For the
production of antibodies rabbits, mice, guinea pigs, goats, sheep, hens and horses are
used, the route of immunization can be intravenous, intramuscular, subcutaneous or
intraperitoneal. The serum collected after immunization is called immune serum or
antiserum, it contains a group of serum proteins also referred to as immunoglobulins.

Initially the immunoanalytical techniques were based on the interaction between antigens and antibodies in solution, leading to the precipitation of the antigen–antibody complex. This precipitation is a measure for the antigen or antibody concentration. These precipitation procedures are suitable for measuring antigen concentrations in the order of mg–mg/ml. However, when the analyte is present in lower concentrations as will be often the case with mycotoxins, other more sensitive methods are needed to measure the complex formation. For these situations the antigen or antibody is labelled for the purpose of counting. Generally, these procedures are meant when the terms "immunochemical methods" or "immuno assays" are used.

In modern immuno assays advantage is taken of two important phenomena: the potential specificity of antibodies to react with a given antigen and, the powerful amplification of the detectability of the antigen–antibody complex, achieved by labelling with indicators. Among others, these indicators (4) can be enzymes, radio–isotopes, fluorescent labels and luminescent labels. After the introduction of Radio Immuno Assay at the end of the 1950's, immuno assays became important tools of analysis in clinical chemistry. For the analysis of food, a much slower sta ccured and the first mycotoxin immuno assay was described in 1976. This rather late ent y is partly due to the fact that mycotoxins are haptens, which means they are not immunogenic and they have to be conjugated with a carrier protein, before immunization can occur to obtain an antiserum. These conjugations can be complicated, because most mycotoxins do not have a suitable reactive group in the molecule to bind with the carrier protein. The lack of suitable reagents precluded a rapid development until the 1980's, when several methods for the preparation of mycotoxin conjugates and aflatoxin conjugates in particular became available. It goes beyond the scope of this presentation t scuss the details of hapten conjugation and production of antibodies against mycotoxins. More important to know is that antisera against some of the mycotoxins, and indicator-labelled mycotoxins have recently become available, although often as part of a test kit only. Most of these have been developed for the determination of aflatoxins.

In the area of mycotoxin research thus far (1987), the use of immuno assays has been limited to Radio Immuno Assay and Enzyme Immuno Assay. In the performance of Radio Immuno Assay and Enzyme Immuno Assay the reversible binding between antigen and antibody plays a central role, as is the case with all immunochemical procedures. The formation of the antigen–antibody lex can be measured by using radio–labelled or enzyme–labelled antigen in competi   a. The application of Radio Immuno Assay has some disadvantages such as limited shelflife activity of the radio isotopes, problems of radioactive waste disposal or licensing requirements and the need of an expensive scintillation counter. These disadvantages probably have led to the fact that only very few Radio Immuno Assays for mycotoxins exist. The technique is much less suitable to be used in the developing countries than Enzyme Immuno Assay which can be applied almost everywhere. Therefore Radio Immuno Assay will not be further discussed in favour of Enzyme Immuno Assay.

In Enzyme Immuno Assay, the formation of the antigen–antibody complex can be measured indirectly by using enzyme-labelled antigen im competition with the antigen to be determined. The quantity of enzyme is a measure for the amount of antigen–antibody complex. It can be measured with chromogenic substrate. At present, most Enzyme Immuno Assays for the determination of mycotoxins are of the type: Enzyme-linked Immunosorbent Assay (ELISA). In ELISA either the antibody or the conjugated antigen is immobilized on a solid support. Often microtitreplates (5) or microtitrestrips are used as solid support. These are transparent and made of polystyrene or polyvinyl chloride. The plates contain 96 small wells, the strips contain 8 or 12 wells. These microtitre plates and strips have several advantages above separate tubes (6). They are easier to handle, they can be washed and read out rather easily, and they are suitable for large series of analyses. The wells of microtitre plates (strips) can be rather uniformly and reproducibly coated with antibody or protein-conjugated antigen. This coating can be realized by simply bringing a buffered aqueous solution with antibody or conjugated antigen in the wells for a period varying from a few hours to one day. The solution is poured out of the wells after coating and the plate is washed a few times with water. After drying, coated plates can be kept in stock for months. In commercial ELISA–kits usually factory-coated plates and strips are supplied.

In the application of ELISA in mycotoxin research several variants exist (7): the competitive assay, the titration assay which is a sequential saturation variant of the competitive assay, and the inhibition assay also called immunometric assay.

In the competition assay (8) a microtitre plate is coated with a known amount of antibody against the mycotoxin looked for. After being washed the test solution, containing an unknown quantity of the mycotoxin, is added together with a known amount of enzyme-labelled mycotoxin. Labelled and non-labelled mycotoxin compete for the active sites of the bound antibody. After incubation the plate is washed again and the captured enzyme is determined by adding chromogenic substrate. The resulting colour or the intensity of the resulting colour can be measured visually or, more precisely, instrumentally with an ELISA reader. In both cases determination of the amount of mycotoxin in the test solution is made by using a series of standards in various concentrations, which have undergone the same procedure. Often, the test solutions are applied in various dilutions if no idea exists about the order of magnitude of the mycotoxin concentration in the test portion. The lower the product concentration of the enzyme reaction, the lower the amount of bound enzyme and the higher the mycotoxin concentration in the test portion. The next slide (9) shows the results of a test in which the intensity of the colour is measured, and a test in which the colour itself is determined. The latter is used in the Agriscreen procedure, a commercial kit for screening foodstuffs and animal feedstuffs for aflatoxin B1.

The titration assay (10) is a sequential saturation variant of the competition assay. A microtitre plate is coated with a known amount of antibody against the mycotoxin looked for. After being washed, the test solution containing an unknown quantity of the mycotoxin is added. The mycotoxin to be measured reacts with a part of the coated antibodies. Then, the unbound antibodies are titrated with enzyme-labelled mycotoxin. The procedure then continues in a similar way as for the competition assay, and also quantitation is carried out in a similar way.

In the inhibition assay (11) the microtitre plate is coated with the mycotoxin and not with the antibody as is done in the competitive and titration assays. The mycotoxin must have been conjugated with a protein at first to make coating possible. The test solution containing an unknown quantity of mycotoxin and a fixed amount of antibody are added to the mycotoxin-coated wells of the microtitre plate. The antibody that has not reacted with mycotoxin from the test-solution is captured by the mycotoxin- coated inside surface of the wells. This captured antibody is usually a rabbit immunoglobulin. After incubation and washing, the plate is incubated with a second (anti-rabbit) antibody, directed against the rabbit antibody and labelled with enzyme. In this way a kind of cascade is obtained: Enzyme-labelled antibody has reacted with anti-mycotoxin antibody which, in turn, has bound to the mycotoxin coated on the well. The captured enzyme is determined by adding chromogenic substrate. The lower the product concentration of the enzyme reaction, the higher the mycotoxin concentration in the test portion. As for the competition and titration ELISA a standard curve is used for determination of the amount of mycotoxin in the test solution. The inhibition ELISA does not require an enzyme labelled mycotoxin and enzyme-linked anti-rabbit antibodies are commercially available, which can be seen as an advantage. However a mycotoxin-protein conjugate is needed to make coating possible to the wells of the microtitre plate.

In addition to the ELISA kits, that make use of microtitre plates or microtitre strips, other solid supports can be used to bind the antibody. A recent development is the "Quick Card" test, a commercial kit that makes use of plastic cards of the size of a credit card (12). In the Quick Card test a controlled amount of anti-aflatoxin antibody is mounted onto each of two parts in the card. In fact this is done in the factory, the card is ready-to-use. A drop of aflatoxin-free control solution is added to the left part and a drop of the test solution is added to the right part. Then enzyme-labelled aflatoxin is added to both card parts, followed by substrate solution. With increasing amounts of aflatoxin, the colour in the port will appear lighter in shade. Conversely, if no aflatoxin is present a strong grey-blue dot will develop in the port (13). The aflatoxin-free control solution will render a dark grey-blue dot. The "Quick Card" test is designed to detect levels of aflatoxins B1, B2, G1 and M1 of approximately 5 or 10 mcg/kg, which is practical from the point of view of most current official tolerances for aflatoxins in foodstuffs. The test provides fast results and requires no equipment or technical experience to perform the test.

The extraction and clean-up procedures needed to perform Enzyme Immuno Assay are generally more simple than those needed to perform Chromatography. Extraction usually occurs with an aqueous solvent e.g. methanol-water, although organic solvents as chloroform are often more efficient. Sometimes a simple defatting step with hexane is applied and usually a column clean-up is not necessary. Unlike many of the extracts, prepared for chromatographic procedures, the final extracts used in Enzyme Immuno Assay are buffered aqueous solutions, because an aqueous environment is needed for the antigen-antibody complex formation to take place.

The simplicity of the ELISA's and the great many samples that can be handled in a day, resulting in relatively low costs per analysis, have made these techniques very valuable for rapid screening under field circumstances. It seems, however, that the ELISA's suffer from larger variability in results that the TLC procedures, although not enough data from collaborative and comparative studies are available as yet to give a full estimation of the merits of ELISA-procedures. Another potential problem is the specificity and selectivity of ELISA's. Many mycotoxins have closely related chemical structures. Because of this, there is a possibility that cross-reactions could occur between antibodies evoked against a certain mycotoxin and other co-occurring toxins within the same group. In some of the commercial aflatoxin-kits this seems to happen, the antibody shows some cross-reactivity with other aflatoxins. It means that a positive result does not give selective information as to the concentration of the separate aflatoxins. This is in contrast to thin layer chromatography, which allows distinguishing between the naturally occurring aflatoxins B1, B2, G1 and G2 .

For the practice of mycotoxin control in Africa, a combination of ELISA and TLC in such a way that ELISA is used for rapid screening and TLC is used for quantitative analysis of positive samples seems, at present, to be a useful and efficient approach.

Slide (1) = Explanation of antigen and antibody
      (2) = Key-lock principle of antigen-antibody reaction
      (3) = Definition of hapten
      (4) = Labels used in immuno assays
      (5) = Picture of ELISA utensils
      (6) = Advantages of microtitre plates above separate tubes
      (7) = ELISA-variants in mycotoxin research
      (8) = Principle of competitive ELISA
      (9) = Results of competitive ELISA
     (10) = Principle of titration ELISA
     (11) = Principle of inhibition ELISA
     (12) = Picture of "Quick Card"
     (13) = Results of "Quick Card" test

4. Method performance characteristics

Analytical chemistry is a practically directed science in which, on the bases of measurement information is obtained as to the qualitative or quantitative composition of substances. An analytical method is a distinct adaptation of a technique for a selected measurement purpose. Methods of analysis have scientific and practical characteristics. The most important scientific characteristics (1) that determine the reliability of the analytical data are the precision, accuracy, detectability, sensitivity and specificity. The practical characteristics (2) encompass the applicability, cost of performance, the time required, the equipment required and the level of training needed. These characteristics determine the utility of the method. It depends on the purposes of the analyst whether the reliability or the utility of the method deserves most attention. For research purposes and compliance activities it may be important that the true value be approached as closely as possible, and practical aspects may be of secondary consideration. Situations are also conceivable in which scientific elegance must be sacrificed for the benefit of practicality, for instance when rapid "go-no-go" tests are required in the field to make a quick decision possible as to whether to accept or reject a lot.

From the literature it is clear that there are many misunderstandings and incorrect usages of the scientific method's performance characteristics. It is therefore appropriate to define these terms.

The sensitivity (3) is the slope of the analytical calibration curve, in other words the change in analytical signal per unit concentration change. It is the value m that we need to know to make a quantification of the analyte on the basis of a certain analytical signal. The sensitivity for the analyte in the final sample extract may not be necessarily equal to the sensitivity for the analyte as present in a simple standard solution. Matrix effects may give rise to an improper calibration of the determinative step of the method of analysis and consequently to estimates of the analyte which are either too high or too low. In analytical chemistry the term "sensitivity" is very often confused with the term "limit of detection", which has another meaning as we shall see later.

A characteristic probably leading to less confusion is the specificity (4): the ability of a method to detect or measure the specific analyte versus similar analytes or interfering compounds. An analytical method is called "fully specific" when it gives an analytical signal solely for one particular component, but is "dead" for all other components, which may also be present in the sample. So, a fully specific procedure gives a zero chance of false-positives. Conventional chromatographic techniques to separate aflatoxins from matrix components are often not fully specific and additional tests need to be done to confirm the presence of aflatoxin in the sample. The most reliable method for this purpose is high-resolution mass spectrometry, but many developing country laboratories will not be equipped with this sophisticated type of apparatus, and therefore more simple techniques have to be applied. Of the various possibilities, to increase the specificity of a method, the derivatization procedures to be carried out directly on the TLC plate or post-column in HPLC-procedures are among the most useful ones.

In addition to these functional characteristics there exist some statistical characteristics as precision and limit of detection and an operational characteristic, the accuracy. Precision and accuracy are often confused with each other, however they have quite different meanings. The precision relates to unavoidable scatter between results obtained by applying a method of analysis in replication either within a laboratory or in different laboratories, whereas the accuracy is a measure of systematic deviation from the true value. The meanings can be illustrated with the help of the following slide (6): A marksman is to fire a number of shots with an old gun trying to hit the bull's eye. The upper left part of the figure shows the first result of his attempt. The results tend to be low, indicating a systematic error and thus a bad accuracy. Besides there is quite some scatter therefore we also conclude the marksman is shooting imprecise. We decide to give the marksman another rifle and repeat the procedure. Now we see again the same scatter, which means again a bad precision but no signs of systematic error, so with the new gun the marksman obtained accurate results. The following part of the picture shows the result of another marks man using the same new gun, and we conclude the scatter is low, thus the precision is good and the accuracy is good as well. Finally the good marksman fires with the old gun: the results are grouped together so there is a good precision, however clearly there is a systematic error, so a bad accuracy. In fact the reason here has been a bent barrel of the old gun.

The precision of the method is usually expressed by the standard deviation of that method or by the relative standard deviation, the so-called coefficient of variation. The precision may relate to the within laboratory error of a method, which can be expressed as the repeatability r or it may relate to the between laboratory error which can be expressed as the reproducibility R. The repeatability r can be defined as the value below which the absolute difference between two single test results obtained with the same method on identical test material under the same conditions may be expected to lie with a specified probability. In the absence of other indications, the probability is 95%. Mathematically the repeatability $r = 2.83 s$ (7), where s = the standard deviation of the test results. In an analogous way the reproducibility R can be defined as the value below which the absolute difference between two single test results obtained with the same method on identical material, but under different conditions (different operators, apparatus, laboratories and/or different times) may be expected to lie with a specified probability. Again, in the absence of other indications, the probability is 95%. Mathematically the reproducibility $R = 2.83 s$ (8), where s = the standard deviation of the test results.

The repeatability and reproducibility of methods of analysis are important characteristics which can serve to verify that the experimental technique of a laboratory is up to standard, or to compare test results obtained within a laboratory or by various laboratories. They give an idea whether observed differences in test results may be significant, or just part of the normal fluctuations.

Information about the precision of a method must be obtained through testing that method in an interlaboratory study. As far as conventional aflatoxin assays are concerned, a fairly good insight is obtained as to the precision aspects of these methods. Horwitz found that aflatoxin assays show reproducibility characteristics that follow the general picture, which is that the interlaboratory precision appears to be a function of concentration and seems to be independent of the nature of the analyte or the technique used for the measurement. In general this precision can be represented by the following equation (9): $C.V.(\%) = 2c$ where c is the concentration expressed as powers of 10 (10). In practice it means that at a level of ca. 10 mg/kg an interlaboratory C.V. occurs at more than 30% and at a level of 0.1 mg/kg this interlaboratory C.V. has gone up to more than 65%.

Further (11), Horwitz observed that the ratio is mostly in between 0.5 and 0.7. A ratio < 0.5 indicates the method to be very personal, analysts can check themselves very well but they cannot check other analysts in other laboratories, a situation asking for reworking of the directions or checking of the reference standards used. A ratio > 0.7 can indicate that individual analysts replications are so poor that they swamp out the between laboratory component.

The following characteristic which deserves some attention is the limit of detection of a method. Again a characteristic which is not defined by every analyst in the same way. Following the IUPAC definition the limit of detection of a method is the lowest concentration level that can be determined to be statistically different from an analytical blank (12). IUPAC states that the limit of detection c is derived from the smallest measure x that can be detected with reasonable certainty for a given analytical procedure. Mathematically $x = x + k.s$ where x is an estimate of the mean value of the blank responses and s is the standard deviation of the blank responses. k is a numerical factor choosen in accordance with the confidence level desired. IUPAC has choosen $k = 3$ which means in practice that there is 90% certainty that a measured signal at x originates from the component searched for, and we call the derived concentration c the limit of detection. The following slide (13) shows the relation between the limit of detection and the sensitivity m: the higher the sensivity the lower the limit of detection. It must be realized that near the limit of detection all quantitative determinations of a substance are rather imprecise. Therefore (14) another criterion has been established by the American Chemical Society at a distance 10 times the standard deviation of the blank away from x. Samples that are measured as having a signal x, where x is more than 10 times the standard deviation of the blank are termed to be in the region of quantitation, which means the concentrations are high enough to do a reasonable quantitation measurement. The range in between 3 times and 10 times the standard deviation of the blank is called the region of detection.

Unfortunately reported data in the literature for the limit of detection and determination seem to be established very subjectively and seldom according to this approach. Some authors relate their reported limit of detection to the lowest amount of aflatoxin just visible on a TLC plate, other establish their limit of detection with standards only or with matrices that cause no serious background. Further complications are the differences in intensities between the various types of UV-lamps and differences in sensitivities between different types of HPLC detectors.

The last characteristic to be discussed is the accuracy (15). This systematic deviation is usually expressed in terms of percentages of recovery. In the practice of conventional aflatoxin assays recoveries of 70-80% are common. The big problem in establishing recoveries is that data are derived in tests with fortified samples. We have to presume that the recovered fraction of naturally present aflatoxin in the sample is equal to that of added aflatoxin. Actually we do not know whether or not all the naturally aflatoxin is amenable to extraction by our initial solvents. The problems may be partly overcome by the use of certified reference materials in which aflatoxins are present through natural way. At least the accuracy of the method under study can be calculated then with the help of a "true value", agreed upon by certification. However, such certified reference materials for aflatoxin determinations are still in a development stage, except for milkpowders with a certified aflatoxin M1 content, which have become available in 1986 through the Community Bureau of Reference (BCR).

The need for mycotoxin reference materials is obvious when the results of mycotoxin interlaboratory studies are considered. Check Sample Programmes for Mycotoxins, as organized by the International Agency for Research on Cancer (16) have shown that large variability in results must be considered more as the norm than the exception, a fact that gives little comfort to those who must either pay for the measurement or who base potentially important decisions upon them. Within the IARC programme samples of agricultural commodities to be analysed for aflatoxins B1, B2, G1 and G2 and milk powders to be analysed for aflatoxin M1 are sent to many participating countries. After sending their analysis results, the participants receive a brief report with the results of preliminary analyses of these samples carried out by three laboratories, choosen for their expertise in aflatoxin assays. At a later stage a full report with all anonymous results is distributed. These reports permit the participating laboratories to judge their performance. Taking part in this IARC Check Sample Programme is free of charge and it is highly recommended, because those working in the field of mycotoxin determination will realize the meaning of Murphy's Law (17):

> Nothing is as easy as it looks.
> Everything takes longer than you expect
> And if anything can go wrong it will
> At the worst possible moment.

VI PROPOSED CURRICULUM FOR A 3-WEEK TRAINING COURSE

This scheme is rather rough, based on previous experiences (see II.5) and subject to adaptation to local situations, personal preferences of the course leader, and newer developments in mycotoxin methodology. If necessary the duration of the course could be somewhat reduced by reducing the number of repetitive exercises.

Day 1 - Personal introductions of participants and course leader
        - Explanation of goal and rough planning of activities.
        - Lecture V.1: Mycotoxins: introduction.

        Practical work:

        - Preparation and handling of aflatoxin standard solutions
        - TLC of aflatoxin B1 standards, inspection under UV light
        - Homework exercises A-C (see IV-annex).

Day 2 - Lecture V.2: TLC techniques.

        Practical work:

        - Preparation of TLC plates.
        - Preparation of TLC developing solvents.
        - Thin layer chromatography of aflatoxins B1, B2, G1, G2 on precoated and selfcoated TLC plates.
        - Identification, Rf values, spot intensities.
        - H2SO4 confirmatory test.
        - Homework exercises D-F (see IV-annex).

Day 3   Practical work:

        - One-dimensional and two-dimensional TLC of extracts (prepared by course leader).
        - Visual interpretation of developed plates.
        - Superimposition of standard spots on extract spots for confirmatory purposes.
        - Estimation of aflatoxin B1 content on TLC plate.
        - H2SO4 confirmatory test.

Day 4   Practical work:

        - One-dimensional and two-dimensional TLC of extracts of agricultural products (extracts prepared by course leader).
        - Visual interpretation of developed plates.
        - Estimation of amounts of aflatoxins B1,B2, G1 and G2 on TLC plate.
        - Calculation of aflatoxins B1, B2, G1 and G2 contents in original samples.
        - Quantitative transfer of extracts from flask to vial.
        - Cleaning of contaminated glassware.
        - Preparation of folded filter papers.

Day 5 - Not programmed, open for repetition of theory or exercises learned at days 1-4, or to be used in case of unforeseen delay.

Day 6   Practical work:

        - Demonstration of various steps of EC procedure.
        - Application of full EC procedure (one- and two-dimensional TLC) for sample provided by course leader.
        - Estimation of aflatoxin B1 content in original sample.
        - Homework exercise G (see IV-annex).

Day 7   Practical work:

- Application of full EC procedure (one- and two-dimensional TLC) for samples provided by course leader.
- Estimation of contents of aflatoxins B1,B2,G1 and G2 in original samples.

Day 8   Practical work:

- Application of full EC procedure (one- and two-dimensional TLC) for samples provided by course leader.
- Estimation of contents of aflatoxins B1,B2,G1 and G2.
- Application of confirmatory tests with H2SO4 and HCl.

Day 9   Same programme as for day 8, however samples of participants choice (local commodities, specific problems).

Day 10   Not programmed, open for repetition of theory or exercises learned at days 6-9, or to be used in case of unforeseen delay.

Day 11   Lecture V.3: ELISA-techniques.

Practical work:

- Demonstration of commercial ELISA-procedure for aflatoxin B1.
- Application of ELISA-procedure for series of aflatoxin B1 standards.
- Application of ELISA-procedure for samples of agricultural products.

Day 12   Lecture V.4: Performance characteristics.

Practical work:

- Application of salt crystal liquefaction test.
- Comparison of TLC and ELISA, applied to same sample.

Day 13   Practical work:

Determination of accuracy and precision of TLC and ELISA procedures by analysing spiked samples in replicate.

Day 14 - Not programmed, open for specific desires, for repetition of theory or exercises learned at days 11-13, or to be used in case of unforeseen delays.
- Distribution of Evaluation Questionnaires.

Day 15 - Individual interviews between participants and course leader.
- Discussion of evaluation questionnaires.
- Closing ceremony.

Questionnaire forms A–E

A. Participant–questionnaire

Name:

Sex: Male/Female

Birthdate:

Educational level:

Experience in aflatoxin B1,B2,G1,G2 assays: Yes, for   years/No.

Experience in aflatoxin M1 assays: Yes, for   years/No.

Present position:

Special interest(s) with respect to mycotoxin methodology:

B.   Facilities-questionnaire

Address of Institute:

Distance from city-centre:

Is the Institute accessable by public transport?

What are the official working-days per week and the official daily working hours?
Are there any public holidays in the proposed training period?

Is there a small conference room available for lectures with possibilities to darken?

Is there a standard size slide projector available, a white projection screen and a blackboard?

Is there enough laboratory space available to train 6 participants at a time?

Are one or more technicians available for technical assistance during the course?

How many fume hoods are available for the course activities?

How is decontamination of glassware (from aflatoxins) normally achieved in the laboratory?

How are organic solvent wastes disposed off in the laboratory?

C.   Reagents—questionnaire

Please indicate whether the following reagents are present in the laboratory where the training course is to take place. All reagents must be of "analytical reagent" quality.

Acetone?

Chloroform, stabilized with 0.5 – 1.0% of ethanol 96%?

n–Hexane?

Methanol?

Anhydrous diethylether, free from peroxides?

Ethyl acetate?

Toluene?

Acetonitrile?

Silica gel, for column chromatography, particle size
   0.05 – 0.20 mm?

Sodium sulphate, anhydrous, granular?

Inert gas, e.g. nitrogen?

Sodium hypochlorite (NaOCl) solution?

Fluted filter papers, Schleicher & Schull, no. 588 or equivalent with 24 cm diameter?

Sodium chloride?

Sodium dodecyl sulphate?

Citric acid?

Phosphoric acid?

Sulphuric acid?

Trifluoroacetic acid?

Acetic acid?

Formic acid?

Hydrochloric acid?

D.   Equipment-questionnaire

Please indicate whether the following items are present in the laboratory where the training course will take place.

TLC-scanner with recorder or integrator? If so, what type?

Micro-analytical balance to weigh accurately at the mg level?

Analytical balance to weigh accurately at the g level?

A high speed precision balance to weigh samples at
 ca 50 – 100 g?

Shaking apparatus for conical flasks with 300–500 ml content?

Rotary vacuum evaporator available with round-bottomed flasks?

UV spectrofotometer equipped with quartz cuvettes? If so, what type?

Longwave UV-lamp, to be used in a dark room? If so, what type and what is its intensity?
(Is a spot of 1.0 ng B1 on a TLC plate clearly visible at a distance of 10 cm from the
lamp?)

Grinding apparatus?

Magnetic stirrer?

Microsyringes? If so, what sizes (volumes) are available and how many of each size?

Spray-unit for TLC (low volume capacity, 5 – 20 ml)?

TLC spreader with 0.25 mm or adjustable outlet slit, inclusive of glass plates, aligning
tray and storage rack?

Oven, adjustable from 70 – 110 C?

Desiccator, with active silica gel desiccant?

Test tubes with screw caps, 50 ml size. If so, how many are available?

Glass columns (internal diameter, 22 mm, length 300 mm), preferably with Teflon cock and
reservoir of 250 ml? If so, how many are available?

Normal laboratory glassware, such as beakers, conical flasks, pipettes, graduates etc. of
different sizes?

TLC tanks with covers? If so, how many of which sizes?

Laboratory sample concentrator (heating block, to accommodate several vials, the contents
of which can be evaporated under N)?
HPLC pump, HPLC silica gel-columns and C18 reverse phase columns,
fluorescence detector connected with recorder/integrator?

Vortex mixer?

Automatic pipettors with disposable tips? If so, what type.

Enzyme Immuno Assay reader? If so, what type.

E. Final participant-questionnaire

Please express your opinion for each of the following questions:

1. The size of the group for the purpose of the activity was:
   too big / just right / too small.

2. Personal contacts with participants and course leader were:
   excellent / normal / poor.

3. The duration of the activity was:
   too long / just right / too short.

4. The quality of the laboratory facilities was:
   very good / sufficient / poor.

5. The balance between theory and practice was:
   optimal/not optimal: too much theory/too much practice.

6. The teaching abilities of the course leader were:
   excellent / sufficient / poor.

7. The home-work exercises were:
   too complicated / just right / too simple

8. The programming of the activity was:
   too rigid / just right / too lax.

9. The overall relevance of the activity to your own work was:
   high / sufficient / low.

10. The following additional remarks and suggestions can be made, which could help in improving the quality of future similar training activities:

THE QUESTIONS ARE ONLY INTENDED TO MAKE YOU FAMILIAR WITH THE CONCEPTS
OFTEN USED IN CALCULATIONS IN MYCOTOXIN ANALYSIS

MICROGRAMME (μg) IS EQUAL TO   NANOGRAMMES (ng)

MILLIGRAMME (mg) IS EQUAL TO   NANOGRAMMES (ng)

GRAMME (g) IS EQUAL TO   KILOGRAMMES (kg)

GRAMME (g) IS EQUAL TO   MICROGRAMMES (μg)

NANOGRAMME (ng) IS EQUAL TO   MICROGRAMMES (μg)

THE QUESTIONS ARE ONLY INTENDED TO MAKE YOU FAMILIAR WITH THE CONCEPTS
OFTEN USED IN CALCULATIONS IN MYCOTOXIN ANALYSIS

MILLIGRAMME (mg) PER KILOGRAMME (kg) EQUALS TO   MICROGRAMME PER GRAMME

MICROGRAMME (μg) PER GRAMME (g) EQUALS TO   MICROGRAMME PER KILOGRAMME

NANOGRAMME (ng) PER GRAMME (g) EQUALS TO   MICROGRAMME PER KILOGRAMME

NANOGRAMME (ng) PER MICROGRAMME (μg) EQUALS TO   MICROGRAMME PER GRAMME

C

THE QUESTIONS ARE ONLY INTENDED TO MAKE YOU FAMILIAR WITH THE CONCEPTS
OFTEN USED IN CALCULATIONS IN MYCOTOXIN ANALYSIS

MILLILITRE (ml) IS EQUAL TO	MICROLITRES (μl)
LITRE (l) IS EQUAL TO	MILLILITRES (ml)
MICROLITRE (μl) IS EQUAL TO	MILLILITRES (ml)
LITRE (l) IS EQUAL TO	MICROLITRES (μl)

THE QUESTIONS ARE ONLY INTENDED TO MAKE YOU FAMILIAR WITH THE CONCEPTS
OFTEN USED IN CALCULATIONS IN MYCOTOXIN ANALYSIS

THE RELATIVE DENSITY OF WATER IS 1.0

MILLILITRE (ml) OF WATER IS WEIGHING	MILLIGRAMMES (mg)
MICROLITRE (μl) OF WATER IS WEIGHING	MILLIGRAMMES (mg)
MILLILITRE (ml) OF WATER IS WEIGHING	MICROGRAMMES (μg)
MILLILITRE (ml) OF WATER IS WEIGHING	GRAMMES (g)

THE QUESTIONS ARE ONLY INTENDED TO MAKE YOU FAMILIAR WITH THE CONCEPTS
OFTEN USED IN CALCULATIONS IN MYCOTOXIN ANALYSIS

THE RELATIVE DENSITY OF CHLOROFORM IS 1.49

MILLILITRE (ml) OF CHLOROFORM IS WEIGHING   GRAMMES (g)

MILLILITRE (ml) OF CHLOROFORM IS WEIGHING   MILLIGRAMMES (mg)

GRAMME (g) OF CHLOROFORM IS EQUAL TO   MILLILITRES (ml)

GRAMME (g) OF CHLOROFORM IS EQUAL TO   MICROLITRES (μl)

THE QUESTIONS ARE ONLY INTENDED TO MAKE YOU FAMILIAR WITH THE CONCEPTS
OFTEN USED IN CALCULATIONS IN MYCOTOXIN ANALYSIS

ASSUME WE HAVE AVAILABLE A WORKING STANDARD SOLUTION OF AFLATOXIN B_1 OF
   μg/ml IN CHLOROFORM;
IF WE SPOT ONTO A TLC PLATE 5-10-15 μl RESPECTIVELY OF THAT STANDARD
HOW MANY NANOGRAMMES AFLATOXIN B_1 HAVE BEEN BROUGHT ONTO THE PLATE
RESPECTIVELY?

THE QUESTIONS ARE ONLY INTENDED TO MAKE YOU FAMILIAR WITH THE CONCEPTS
OFTEN USED IN CALCULATIONS IN MYCOTOXIN ANALYSIS

ASSUME YOU HAVE EXTRACTED 50 g OF PEANUTS AND THE EXTRACT WAS FURTHER
ANALYZED ACCORDING TO THE EC-PROCEDURE. YOUR ENDVOLUME IS 2 ml;
OF THAT ENDVOLUME YOU SPOT ONTO THE TLC PLATE μl.
THE AFLATOXIN B_1 SPOT ON THE PLATE OF YOUR EXTRACT HAS THE SAME
FLUORESCENCE INTENSITY AS   ng AFLATOXIN B_1.
HOW MUCH AFLATOXIN B_1 IS PRESENT IN THE ENDVOLUME OF YOUR SAMPLE
EXTRACT (in ng)?
WHAT IS THE AFLATOXIN B_1 CONTENT OF YOUR SAMPLE (μg/kg)?

Annex III

Bibliography

ACS Subcommittee on Environmental Analytical Chemistry (1980) Anal. Chem. 52, 2242.

Alfin-Slater R.B., Aftergood, L., Hernandez, H.J., Sterm, E. and Melnick, D. (1969), J. Am. Oil Chem. Soc. 46, 493.

Allcroft, R. and Carnaghan, R.B.A. (1963). Vet Rec., 75, 259.

AOAC (1984). In: Official Methods of Analysis of the Association of Official Analytical Chemists, Horwitz, W. (Ed.), Arlington, Virginia, USA, ISBN 0-935584-24-2, p. 477.

Asplin, F.D. and Carnaghan, R.B.A. (1961). Vet. Rec., 73, 1215.

Beljaars, P.R., Verhülsdonk, C.A.H., Paulsch, W.E. and Liem, D.H. (1973). J. Assoc. Off. Anal. Chem., 56, 1444.

Bendele A.M., Carlton W.W., Krogh P. and Lillehoj E.B. (1985). J. Natl. Cancer Inst. 75, 733.

Biermann, A. and Terplan G., (1980 A) Inaugural Dissertation zur Erlangung der tiermedizinischen Doktorwurde der Tierarztlichen Fakultat der Ludwig-Maximilians-Universitat Munchen", F.R.G.

Biermann, A. and Terplan G., (1980 B). Arch. Lebensmittel hyg. 31, 51.

Brown, R.F., Wildman, J.D. and Eppley, R.M. (1968), J. Assoc. Off. Anal. Chem., 51, 905.

Burmeister, H.R. and Hesseltine, C.W. (1966). Appl. Microbiol., 14, 403.

Burmeister, H.R. and Hesseltine, C.W. (1970). Appl. Microbiol., 20, 437.

Butler W.H. and Barnes J.M. (1968) Food Cosmet. Tox. 6, 135.

Carnaghan, R.B.A., Hartley, R.D. and O'Kelly, J. (1963). Nature, 200, 1101.

Chu, F.S. (1984) J. Food Prot. 47, 562.

Chu, F.S. (1983). In: Proc. Int. Symp. Mycotoxins, Cairo, Egypt, September 1981, p. 177.

Chung, C.W., Trucksess, M.W., Giles, A.L. and Friedman, L. (1974). J. Assoc. Off. Anal. Chem., 57, 1121.

Clements, N.L. (1968). J. Assoc. Off. Anal. Chem., 51, 1192.

Commission of the European Communities (1976). Off. J. Europ. Comm. L102.

Crosby, N.T. and Hunt, D.C. (1978). In: Proc. 3rd Meeting on Mycotoxins in Animal Disease, Weybridge, U.K., April 1978, p. 34.

Cucullu, A.F., Lee, L.S. Mayne, R.Y. and Goldblatt, L.A. (1966). J. Am. Oil Chem. Soc., 43, 89.

Davis, N.D. and Diener, U.L. (1979). J. Appl. Biochem., 1, 123.

Davis, N.D. and Diener, U.L. (1980). J. Assoc. Off. Anal. Chem., 63, 107.

DeVries, J.W. de and Chang, H.L. (1982). J. Assoc. Off. Anal. Chem., 65, 206.

Dickens, J.W. and Satterwhite J.B. (1969). Food Technol., 23, 950.

Dickens, J.W. (1977). J. Am. Oil Chem. Soc., 54, 225A.

Dickens, J.W. (1978). In: Gesundheitsgefahrdung durch Aflatoxine, Poiger, H. (Ed.), Arbeitstagung Zurich, Marz, 1978. Eigen Verlag Institut fur Toxikologie der ETH unter der Universitat Zurich, Schwerzenbach, Switzerland, p. 258.

Dil L.A.G. (1986) Dissertation submitted to the University of Zambia in fulfilment of the requirements of the degree of Master of Science in Chemistry, Zambia.

Egmond, H.P. van, Paulsch, W.E., Deijll, E. and Schuller, P.L. (1980). J. Assoc. Off. Anal. Chem., 63, 110.

Egmond H.P. van (1987) working document Myc. 87/9.1 and 9.2. Second Joint FAO/WHO/UNEP International Conference on Mycotoxins, Bangkok.

Egmond H.P. van, Paulsch W.E. and Sizoo E.A. (1987) J. Food Add. Contam. – in press –

El-Nakib, O., Pestka J.J. and Chu F.S. (1981). J. Assoc. Off. Anal. Chem. 64, 1077.

Eppley, R.M. (1966). J. Assoc. Off. Anal. Chem., 49, 1218.

Francis, O.J. (1979). J. Assoc. Off. Anal. Chem., 62, 1182.

Frémy, J.M. and Chu F.S. (1984). J. Assoc. Off. Anal. Chem. 67, 1098.

Friesen M.D. and Garren L. (1982). J. Assoc. Off. Anal. Chem. 65.

Haghighi, B., Thorpe, C.W., Pohland, A.E. and Barnett, R. (1981). J. Chrom., 206, 101.

Harder, W.O. and Chu F.S. (1979). Experientia 35/8, 1104.

Heathcote J.G. and Hibbert J.R. (1978) In: Aflatoxin: Chemical and Biological Effects. Elsevier Scientific Publ. Co. New York, USA.

Hesseltine C.W. (1986). In: Mycotoxins and Phycotoxins, P.S. Steyn and R. Vleggaar (Eds.), Elsevier Science Publishers B.V. Amsterdam, ISBN 0-444- 42632-9, p. 1.

Holaday, C.E. (1968). J. Am. Oil Chem. Soc., 45, 680.

Holaday, C.E. (1976). J. Am. Oil Chem. Soc., 53, 603.

Holaday, C.E. (1980). J. Am. Oil Chem. Soc., 57, 491A.

Horwitz W., Kamps L.R. and Boyer K.W. (1980). J. Assoc. Off. Anal. Chem. 63, 1344.

Horwitz W. and Albert R. (1981). The reliability of aflatoxin assays. Lecture presented ad the 85th Annual Conference of the Association of Food and Drug Officials, June 15, 1981, St. Louis, Missouri, USA.

Hsieh, D.S.P. (1986) In: Mycotoxins and Phycotoxins. P.S. Steyn and R. Vleggaar (Eds), Elsevier Science Publishers, B.V. Amsterdam, The Netherlands, ISBN 0-444-42632-9, p. 447.

International Diagnostics (1987). EZ-screen Aflatoxin Quick Card. Directions for use. International Diagnostic Systems Corporation, St. Joseph, Michigan, USA.

International Standard Organization (1981). International standard ISO 5725.

Jackman, R. (1985) J. Sci. Food Agric. 36, 685.

Jemmali, M. (1977). Arch. Inst. Past. Tunis, 3-4, 249.

Kang, A.S., Morgan, M.R.A. and Chan, H.W.S. (1984) In: Proc. of the Vth Meeting on Mycotoxins in Animal and Human Health, Edinburgh, U.K. 1984, p. 80.

Kiermeier, F. and Groll, D. (1970). Z. Lebensmitt. - Untersuch., 142, 120.

Kleinau, G. (1981). Die Nahrung, 25, K9.

Kmieciak, S. (1976). Z. Lebensmitt. Unters.-Forsch., 160, 321.

Krogh. P. (1974). In: Endemic Nephropathy. A. Puchlew, I. Dinev, B. Milev and D. Doichinov, Eds. Publishing House of the Bulgarian Academy of Sciences, Sofia, Bulgaria, p. 266.

Krogh P. (1977) In: Mycotoxins in Human and Animal Health. J.V. Rodricks, C.W. Hesseltine and M.A. Mehlman (Eds). Pathotox Publishers, Park Forest South, Illinois, U.S.A., ISBN 0-930376-00-5, p. 489.

Langone, J.J. and Vunakis, H. van (1976). J. Natl. Cancer Inst., 56, 591.

Lee, S. and Chu, F.S. (1981). J. Assoc. Off. Anal. Chem., 64, 156.

Lee, S. C. and Chu, F.S. (1984). J. Assoc. Off. Anal. Chem. 67, 45.

Long, G.L. and Winefordner (1983). Anal. Chem. 55, 712 A.

Manabe, M., Goto, T. and Maisuura, S. (1978). Agric. Biol. Chem., 42, 2003.

Märtlbauer, E. and Terplan G. (1985) "Ein hochempfindlicher heterologer enzymimmunologischer Nachweis von Aflatoxin M1 in Milch und Milchpulver". Archiv fur Lebensmittelhyg. 36, 53.

Mirocha, C.J., Schauerhamer, B. and Pathre, S.V. (1974). J. Assoc. Off. Anal. Chem., 57, 1104.

Morgan, M.R.A., Matthew, J.A., Mc Nerney, R. and Chan, H.W.S. (1982). In: Proc. Vth Int. IUPAC Symp. Mycotoxins and Phyco toxins, Vienna, Austria. September 1982, p. 32.

Morgan, M.R.A., McNerney, R., Chan, H.W.S. and Anderson P.H. (1986) J. Sci. Food Agric. 37, 475.

Neogen Corporation (1986). "Agri-screen for Aflatoxin B detection". Directions for use. Neogen Corporation, Lansing, Michigan U.S.A.

Nixon J.E., Sinnhuber, R.O., Lee, D.J., Landers M.K. and Harr J.R. (1974). J. Natl. Cancer Inst. 53, 453.

Northolt, M.D., Egmond, H.P. van, Soentoro, P.S.S. and Deijll, W.E. (1980). J. Assoc. Off. Anal. Chem., 63, 115.

Northolt M.D. and Heuvelman C.J. (1982) J. Food Prot. 45, 537.

Northolt M.D. and Egmond H.P. van (1982) In: Proc. 4th Meeting on Mycotoxins in Animal Disease, Weybridge, U.K., April 1981, p. 106.

Northolt M.D. and Soentoro P.S.S. (1984). In: Introduction to Food Borne Fungi. R.A. Samson, E.S. Hoekstra, C.A.N. van Oorschot (Eds.) Centraal Bureau voor Schimmelcultures, Baarn, the Netherlands, ISBN 90-70351-03, p. 212.

OECD (1982). In: Handbook on rapid detection of mycotoxins. OECD, Paris, France. January 1982, p. 13.

Park, D.L., Hart, L.P., Miller, B.M., Yang, G., McVey, J., Page, S.W., Pestka J. and Brown, L.H. (1987). Submitted to J. Assoc. Off. Anal. Chem.

Patterson, D.S.P. and Roberts, B.A. (1979). J. Assoc. Off. Anal. Chem., 62, 1265.

Paulsch, W.E., Egmond, H.P. van and Schuller, P.L. (1982). In: Proc. Vth Int. IUPAC Symp. Mycotoxins and Phycotoxins, Vienna, Austria. September 1982, p. 40.

Pero, R.W., Harvan, D., Owens, R.G. and Snow, J.P. (1972). J. Chrom., 65, 501.

Pestka J.J., Lee S.C., Lau H.P. and Chu, F.S. (1981) J. Am. Oil Chem. Soc. 58, 940A.

Pohland, A.E., Sanders, K. and Thorpe, C.W. (1970). J. Assoc. Off. Anal. Chem., 53, 692.

Pons, W.A. and Goldblatt, L.A. (1965). J. Am. Oil Chem. Soc. 42, 471.

Pons, W.A. (1976). J. Assoc. Off. Anal. Chem., 59, 101.

Romer, T.R. (1975). J. Assoc. Off. Anal. Chem. 58, 500.

Romer, T.R. and Campbell, A.D. (1976). J. Assoc. Off. Anal. Chem., 59, 110.

Schoental, R. and White, A.F. (1965). Nature, 205, 57.

Schuller, P.L., Stoloff, L. and Egmond, H.P. van. (1983). In: Proc. Int. Symp. Mycotoxins, Cairo, Egypt, September 1981, p.111.

Schuller P.L., Verhülsdonk C.A.H. and Paulsch W.E. (1973) Pure Appl. Chem. 35, 291.

Scott, W.J. (1957). Adv. Food Res. 7, 83.

Scott, P.M., Walbeek, W. van, Kennedy, B. and Anyeti, D. (1972). J. Agric. Food. Chem., 20, 1103.

Scott, P.M. (1981). In: Trace Analysis-1 (Ed. J.F. Lawrence), Academic Press, London, U.K. p.193.

Scott, P.M. (1984). J. Assoc. Off. Anal. Chem. 67, 366.

Seiber, J.N. and Hsieh, D.P.H. (1973). J. Assoc. Off. Anal. Chem., 56, 827.

Smith, R.H. and McKernan, W. (1962), Nature, 195, 1301.

Speyers G.J.A., Franken, M.A.M., Leeuwen F.X.R. van (1987). Submitted to Food Chem. Toxicol.

Speyers G.J.A., Franken M.A.M., Leeuwen F.X.R. van, Egmond, H.P. van, Boot, R., Loeber, J.G. (1988). Submitted to Food Chem. Toxicol.

Stack, M. and Rodricks, J.V. (1971). J. Assoc. Off. Anal. Chem., 54, 86.

Stoloff, L. (1977) In: Mycotoxins in Human and Animal Health, J.V. Rodricks, C.W. Hesseltine, M.A. Mehlman (Eds.) Pathotox Publishers, Inc., Park Forest South IL, USA, ISBN 0-930376-00-5, p.7.

Stubblefield R.D. (1979). J. Am. Oil Chem. Soc. 56, 800.

Stubblefield, R.D. (1979). J. Assoc. Off. Anal. Chem., 62, 201.

Stubblefield, R.D. and Shotwell, O.L. (1981). J. Assoc. Off. Anal. Chem., 64, 964.

Takahashi, D.M. (1977). J. Chrom., 131, 147.

Thorpe, C.W., Ware G.M. and Pohland, A.E. (1982). In: Proc. Vth Int. IUPAC Symp. Mycotoxins and Phycotoxins, Vienna, Austria, September 1982, p. 52.

Trucksess, M.W. (1976). J. Assoc. Off. Anal. Chem., 59, 722.

Trucksess, M.W., Nesheim, S. and Eppley, R.M. (1984). J. Assoc. Off. Anal. Chem. 67, 40.

Tuinstra, L.G.M.Th. and Haasnoot, W. (1982). Fres. Z. Anal. Chem., 312, 622.

Umeda, M. (1971). Japan. J. Exp. Med., 41, 195.

Umeda, M. (1977). In: Mycotoxins in Human and Animal Health, J.V. Rodricks, C.W. Hesseltine and M.A. Mehlman, (Eds), Pathotox Pub- lishers, Park Forest South Illinois, USA ISBN 0-930376-00-5, p. 713.

Van Rensburg S.J. (1986) In: Mycotoxins and Phycotoxins, P.S. Steyn and R. Vleggaar (Eds), Elsevier Science Publishers B.V. Amsterdam, the Netherlands. ISBN 0-444-42632-9, p. 483.

Velasco, J. (1970). J. Assoc. Off. Anal. Chem. 53, 611.

Verhülsdonk, C.A.H., Schuller, P.L. and Paulsch, W.E. (1977). Zeszyty Problemowe Postepow Nauk Rolniczych, 189, 277.

Verrett, M.J., Winbush, J., Reynaldo, E.F. and Scott, W.F. (1973). J. Assoc. Off. Anal. Chem., 56, 901.

Waart, J. de., Aken, F. van, and Pouw, H. (1972). Zbl. Bakt. Hyg. I. Abt. Orig., 222, 96.

Wagstaffe, P.J. (1987) In: Proc. Symposium Aflatoxin and edible Peanuts, Leatherhead, U.K. October 1986, p 24.

Watson, D.H. and Lindsay, D.G. (1982). J. Sci. Food Agric., 33, 59.

Whitaker, T.B. (1977). Pure and Appl. Chem., 49, 1709.

Whitaker, T.B., Dickens, J.W. and Monroe, R.J. (1980). J. Am. Oil Chem. Soc., 57, 269.

WHO, (1980). Environmental Health Criteria Document 11: Mycotoxins, ISBN 92-4-254-071-4.

Wiseman H.G., Jacobson W.C. and Harmeyer W.C. (1967) J. Assoc. Off. Anal. Chem 50, 982.

Wogan G.N. (1973) In: Methods in Cancer Research, H. Bush, (Ed.) Academic Press, New York USA, p. 309.

Wogan G.N. (1974) Food Cosmet. Tox. 12, 681.

Zimmerli, B. (1977). J. chromatogr. 131, 458.

Tipo-lito SAGRAF - Napoli